LB
2343
.R49
1995

Riedinger, Edward
Anthony, 1944-

Where in the world to
learn.

$55.00

DATE			

Where
in the World
to Learn

Recent Titles in
The Greenwood Educators' Reference Collection

Planning in School Administration: A Handbook
Ward Sybouts

School Law for the 1990s: A Handbook
Robert C. O'Reilly and Edward T. Green

Handbook of Academic Advising
Virginia N. Gordon

Handbook for the College and University Career Center
Edwin L. Herr, Jack R. Rayman, and Jeffrey W. Garis

Handbook of Cooperative Learning Methods
Shlomo Sharan, editor

Handbook of College Teaching: Theory and Applications
Keith W. Prichard and R. McLaran Sawyer, editors

The Training and Development of School Principals: A Handbook
Ward Sybouts and Frederick C. Wendel

Multiculturalism in the College Curriculum: A Handbook of Strategies and Resources
for Faculty
Marilyn Lutzker

WHERE IN THE WORLD TO LEARN

A Guide to Library and Information Science for International Education Advisers

Edward A. Riedinger

The Greenwood Educators' Reference Collection

GREENWOOD PRESS
Westport, Connecticut • London

Library of Congress Cataloging-in-Publication Data

Riedinger, Edward Anthony.
    Where in the world to learn : a guide to library and information
science for international education advisers / Edward A. Riedinger.
      p. cm.—(The Greenwood educators' reference collection,
ISSN 1056–2192)
    Includes bibliographical references (p.) and index.
    ISBN 0–313–28703–1 (alk. paper)
    1. Counseling in higher education. 2. Faculty advisors.
3. International education—Information services. I. Title.
II. Series.
LB2343.R49   1995
378.1'94—dc20   94–42728

British Library Cataloguing in Publication Data is available.

Library of Congress Catalog Card Number: 94–42728
ISBN: 0–313–28703–1
ISSN: 1056–2192

First published in 1995

Greenwood Press, 88 Post Road West, Westport, CT 06881
An imprint of Greenwood Publishing Group, Inc.

Printed in the United States of America

The paper used in this book complies with the
Permanent Paper Standard issued by the National
Information Standards Organization (Z39.48–1984).

10 9 8 7 6 5 4 3 2

Grateful acknowledgment is made to *The Advising Quarterly* for permission to reprint sections in
Chapter 1 of this book from my article in that review, "Overseas Educational Advising: An
International Information Service" (no. 20, Spring 1992, pp. 18–24).

To the advisees and advisers whom I have advised,
This work is a summation.

To the advisers whose foresight sees the need to
develop advising as a professional information service,
This work is a preparation.

And with admiration and gratitude
To the Honorable J. William Fulbright.

In traveling, a man must carry knowledge with him if he would bring knowledge home.

—Samuel Johnson

Les voyages donnent une très grande entendue à l'esprit: on sort du cercle des préjuges de son pays, et l'on n'est guère propre à se charger de ceux des étrangers.

—Montesquieu

Contents

Figures

Preface and Acknowledgments

My thinking about advising offices as libraries began in the early 1980s after my initial year as director of the Fulbright advising office in Rio de Janeiro, Brazil. However, the idea that there was a need for a handbook or guide applying library and information science principles and practices to advising did not begin to emerge until 1984, when I read Gary Althen's *The Handbook of Foreign Student Advising*. This book made me perceive that something as insightful and substantive needed to be developed for overseas advising, and for advising in international education in general.

By 1986 I decided to improve my own skills in administering information services by enrolling for a semester in the School of Library and Information Studies at the University of California, Berkeley. I am grateful to the Fulbright Commission of Brazil for granting me official leave to attend the school. I am most grateful to the school itself, which gave impetus to learning the techniques of information accumulation and retrieval, in which its faculty, students, laboratories, and libraries excelled. Even more, it stimulated challenging the "information age" and its absolutes.

A number of librarians, advisers, and personnel in international education have given me insight and support in refining the development of advising as a professional information service. I am grateful to my library colleagues at Ohio State University for their expertise and assistance. Moreover, I thank the library administration for giving me the time to complete this book through research leave.

I am indebted to the editorial staff of *The Advising Quarterly*, especially its head, Juleann Fallgatter, for all the resources in advising which they have developed and so generously shared. I also thank the many advisers in Brazil, Latin America, and on OSEASNet (the worldwide electronic communications network of overseas educational advisers [OSEAS]) for their support and interest in my efforts.

I wish to recognize the work of John Hopkins of the University of Tampere (Finland) in establishing the electronic OSEAS database (which can be reached electronically via the use of telnetting to either gopher.colostate.edu or gopher. csc.fi). It contains directory information for almost a thousand educational advisers, in over 150 countries, for study in the United States. Indeed, the current and future members of this group are the core section of advisers I hope to reach in this work.

Among advisers I especially wish to recognize my predecessor at the Fulbright advising office in Rio de Janeiro, Freya James. Freya founded the office in 1969 and headed it until 1979. She left a solid base from which to expand, and several of the lessons I learned from her are presented here. I also salute the members of my advising office staff who were cooperative and active in the development of advising. Their work too is passed on here.

Further, I wish to recognize three key agencies for their support and contributions for advising in terms of sponsoring training, developing materials, and aiding professional organization: the Advising, Teaching, and Specialized Programs Division of the United States Information Agency (USIA); the International Education Office of the College Board; and NAFSA: Association of International Educators. Finally, I thank the European overseas educational advisers (OSEAS/Europe), who in 1991 invited me to speak at their third regional conference, in Montpellier, France. That encounter prompted me to begin this book, and the first chapter is an adaptation of my paper at that conference.

When I think of acknowledgments in the deeper sense, the influences that molded my thinking and work in advising go back quite far. I think of my father, and the model of order and organization he conveyed. I think of my mother, and her attention to detail, together with her emphasis on honesty and integrity. My experience as a college student working in the Indianapolis Public Library also showed me how a library or information system was coordinated from its central operation to branches.

Moreover, as a seminarian for the priesthood, I saw the Catholic Church functioning as a uniform, global operation through its coordination of dioceses and hierarchy. Indeed, Catholicism gave me an architecture of thought in which one saw the significance of a phenomenon as a whole, yet at the same time was aware of all of the phenomenon's minute details of operation. Grasping the whole meant knowing detail. I had thought of being a missionary, and thus believed that thought should be realized in action. Thought and action were sides of the same coin. Further, my tendency toward catholic, encyclopedic inquiry imbued me for advising, in which one has to be universally curious and resolute in knowing something about any field of knowledge or profession.

Although I worked or visited advising offices around the globe, my primary advising experience took place in Brazil with Brazilians. That country has recently endured much economic and political turmoil, but I truly remember most of my experiences there as idyllic. Without equal are Brazil's openness of spirit, sunlit richness of nature, and air of serene languor.

I first went to Brazil in 1971 to live in Rio de Janeiro and begin field research for my doctoral dissertation at the University of Chicago. Previously I had traveled only in Europe, and lived abroad in England, at Oxford University. My first view of Brazil from the descending plane in the morning light was of forbidding stretches of brushland and reddish earth. After the plane landed in Rio, this forbidding aspect continued. Passengers wandered in a dingy warehouse of an airport (since replaced by a sleek, modern complex). The taxi ride into the city took me through the accustomed, anonymous sprawl of a metropolitan periphery. Where, I asked myself, was the wonder that Rio de Janeiro was supposed to be?

Then the car came to the downtown and moved along the neighborhoods of the bay and ocean. Suddenly the classical, tropical splendor of Rio arched before me. Delicate grey mountain pinnacles rose from amid the cityscape. Lush vegetation wrapped the base of the peaks and swept up to drape the mountainsides. The water and beaches of the bay and then the ocean sinuously bordered this backdrop, and everything was bathed in triumphant sunlight under the banner of an azure sky. It was then that I knew a wonderful adventure awaited me. I was in love with Rio de Janeiro there and then, and seemingly forever. Never in the sixteen years that I lived in the city did I not marvel at that unique urban landscape as I rode or walked through it. No city in the world has such a fathomless allure of beauty. (Paris, I recognize, has its exceptional, extraordinary allure; but its beauty is due not to intricate dimensions of intermingled nature, but to the elegant detail of man.)

I emphasize Brazil's allure because I do not believe I would have been as dedicated to advising had it not been for the fact that I could apply my particular background and character to an environment and for a people that so enchanted me. Indeed, it seems to me that the very nature of overseas advising requires that one desire to match the value of international education with the value one respects in the overseas environment. This requirement is especially true if advisers are not native to the country in which they are doing advising.

Even today, more than a half dozen years after leaving Brazil, if an American student asks me about a study opportunity at a university or about financial aid from some organization, I remember Brazilian students who asked me similar questions. I recall their tan, attentive faces. For them to study in California was to go to wonderland, and obtaining a *bolsa* (Portuguese for scholarship or any type of financial aid) the magical means to bear them there. Education professionals in Brazil were very innovative and eagerly supportive of my interest in expanding and improving overseas advising services in their country.

A Portuguese word for acknowledgment is *homenagem* (giving homage, recognition). I close this preface by paying *homenagem* with a poem of mine, dedicated to that rich country and environment, which gave me such abundant inspiration and opportunity for developing advising.

BRASIL

Sunlight.
And green.
Then sunlight on leaves and
    through leaves.
And sand and water and mountains.
Then houses and quiet voices,
A breeze from the sea
    and distant strumming.
Then love and then night.

And sunlight.
Then green . . .

Brasil, viaticum for memory.

Abbreviations

ACE	American Council on Education
ALA	American Library Association
AMIDEAST	America-Mideast Educational and Training Services
BIP	*Books in Print*
CGFNS	Commission on Graduates of Foreign Nursing Schools
CGS	Council of Graduate Schools
DDC	Dewey Decimal Classification
ECFMG	Educational Commission for Foreign Medical Graduates
ETS	Educational Testing Service
GMAT	Graduate Management Admission Test
GRE	Graduate Record Examination
IIE	Institute of International Education
IREX	International Research and Exchanges Board
ISBN	International Standard Book Number
ISIS	Integrated Set of Information Systems
ISSN	International Standard Serial Number
LASPAU	Latin American Scholarship Program of American Universities (affiliated with Harvard University)
MRB	Minimum Reference Bookshelf
NAFSA	NAFSA: Association of International Educators
OCLC	Online Computer Library Center

OSEAS	Overseas Educational Advisers
SAT	Scholastic Assessment Test
SLA	Special Libraries Association
SRC	Select Reference Collection
TOEFL	Test of English as a Foreign Language
UDC	Universal Decimal Classification
UNESCO	United Nations Educational, Scientific, and Cultural Organization
USIA	United States Information Agency
USIS	United States Information Service

Introduction

This book is primarily a guide for international education advisers (those who give orientation for study in another country) to skills in library and information science, so that they may begin to achieve expertise as information professionals. This focus results from my experience as the head of an overseas educational advising operation in Brazil from 1979 to 1988.

It concentrates on material for U.S. overseas educational advisers and for multinational advisers (those who advise for study in various countries) who have American education as part of their responsibilities. The acronym OSEAS has come to describe such advisers as a group. However, this book's objective includes all advisers working in international education. Thus, the principles delineated in this guide are considered useful for study abroad advisers, meaning those who orient students and scholars in this country about education opportunities abroad, and for, again, multinational advisers in their responsibilities outside American education. All international education advisers need to know the operations which will make their advising offices function as professional information services.

The materials indicated in this guide are relevant primarily to educational advisers abroad orienting about American education. Its principles, nonetheless, apply to the spectrum of international education advisers: U.S. overseas, multinational, and study abroad. In this respect, therefore, while I have concentrated on needs represented by U.S.-focused advisers, I hope that in the future additional guides may be written, supplementing this work by describing the educational orientation materials of countries other than the United States. Such guides will not have to repeat the general principles and many practices of library and information sciences elaborated here, but will only have to indicate the educational orientation resources for other countries. (To examine a tentative effort in this regard, see Appendix B.)

What are the principles of this work relevant to all advisers in international education? All must be aware of advising as an information system: (1) gathering, (2) organizing, (3) communicating, and (4) managing information.

With an awareness of these stages in the information continuum, an adviser must then learn the techniques operable and resources available for each of these stages. In order to carry out the stages of an information system as a professional service, one must carry out the fundamental principles and practices of library and information science: (1) collection development, (2) cataloging, (3) reference service, and (4) library and information management.

If the heart of advising is to communicate information, the substance of it is achieved only when professional information service practices are incorporated. To put substance into advising, it is necessary that its practitioners be information professionals.

I emphasize awareness of library operations because in visiting many overseas educational centers around the world during the past decade I was always struck on first entering them by their resemblance to small, specialized libraries. I visited centers from Hong Kong to Cairo and from London to Santiago; I administered the Fulbright advising office in Rio de Janeiro, and aided in setting up or remodeling many within Brazil and throughout South America. That initial library impression always remained with me, for the heart, the substance, of advising involves specialized information or library work.

I also found that while advisers were invariably quite dedicated people, enjoying and committed to their work of aiding others to know about foreign study or research, they usually had no skills in library or information center operations. They came from varied educational and professional backgrounds: teaching, history, business, counseling, nursing, and numerous other fields. Frequently they were unaware of the concepts of librarianship or of information science and of their relevance to advising centers. As a result, they were often frustrated or even oblivious to how they could acquire the skills to obtain and organize the information they often wanted for their advisees.

The techniques of library and information science conveyed herein are those applicable to the practices of small and special libraries, administered by advisers without training in librarianship. The advising centers are considered libraries which are small because of the size of their staff, collection, budget, and public relative to large operations such as major university or metropolitan public libraries. They are considered special because their user needs are focused on particular information objectives: study, training, or research outside one's own country (in this case, the United States).

I have taken from library and information science what I think is most basic and applicable to advising centers as small, special libraries. This guide, therefore, emphasizes collection development, cataloging, reference service, and library and information management. However, though small as libraries, advising centers themselves vary in size, ranging from those with a one-person, part-time adviser to operations with a dozen advisers, support staff, and volunteers.

The smaller the advising operation, the more selective will be the needs from this guide. A one-person advising center will probably only have need for the information on collection development and reference service and require only notions about cataloging and management. In principle, the larger the advising center, the more applicable will be all the material in this guide.

Moreover, I believe beginning advisers, as all novices, will benefit more from this work than the more experienced. The latter will have learned in their advising experience some of the lessons contained here. They will, however, appreciate being able to refine their advising along lines of systematic information service operations. Both newer and more experienced advisers will appreciate the perception and organization of advising within the precepts of librarianship, a profession going back millennia, to the beginning of the written word.

The reason for this guide is to ensure substance in advising through professional information practices. Its assumption is that the needs of those seeking information about study in another country are as specialized as those of inventors seeking information in patent libraries, lawyers in law libraries, or doctors in medical libraries. The conviction of this book is that overseas study information needs are as worthy of professional attention and development as the currents and flow of international education in the modern world are powerful.

Where
in the World
to Learn

1

Advising as an Information Service

TOWARD A RATIONALE AND METHODOLOGY FOR
DEVELOPING ADVISING AS THE PROFESSIONAL
INFORMATION ARM OF INTERNATIONAL EDUCATION

In the past decade and a half overseas educational advising has achieved remarkable definition and organization. Meetings of advisers in national or regional conferences and workshops now occur regularly around the globe in such
countries as Argentina, Brazil, Britain, Chile, France, Hungary, Malaysia, Russia, and the former Yugoslavia. The service of informing and orienting students
and scholars around the world on study or research opportunities in the United
States is now a recognized service supported by U.S. government policy. Moreover, numerous other governments, particularly France, Britain, and Germany,
maintain such services abroad for their own educational systems. The number
of U.S. advising offices has increased in all regions of the world, the advisers
in them receive more extensive and regular training, and the materials in these
offices are now greater and more varied.

In the midst of this rapid growth, it becomes crucial to understand the larger
historical context from which overseas educational advising is emerging. We
must understand this context in order to perceive the profound historical relevance of advising and, thereby, to attain the level of professional development
and resources necessary to fulfill this role.

Two major current developments are particularly significant in considering
the historical context of advising: the phenomenon of an information society
and the internationalization of the globe. International education advising offers
a key service relevant to both these developments, providing information about

study and research in other countries and about international activities in education.

As the past decade saw the emergence and growth of educational advising, the present and coming decades must see it become an ever more reliable professional information service. It must become the information arm or division of international education.

Why and how will this next stage of development occur? To answer this question, we must examine the elements of advising's historical context: (1) the establishment of the information society or age, (2) the internationalization of the globe and the role of education in this process, and (3) the role of advising in relation to these developments.

INFORMATION SOCIETY

Information can be defined as data (that is, raw information) or as knowledge (meaning structured, significant information). Information, then, can be associated with both the product itself and with the means of producing it. The terms "information society" and "information age" suggest that our current age, history since the end of World War II, has come to be dominated by information.

How and where has the perception emerged that information dominates modern life to the extent that it defines an age? To answer this question we must review some elementary distinctions of economics.

One traditional way to describe an economy is by type of production, dividing it into sectors. The "primary sector" refers to cultivating or extracting raw materials (in such activities, for example, as agriculture or mining). The "secondary sector" refers to activities whereby raw materials are processed or manufactured (farm products becoming packaged foods, iron ore becoming steel beams). The "tertiary sector" refers to services (activities such as medicine, insurance, tourism, or banking).

Economies are usually a mixture of the above sectors but are dominated by one of them. Many countries of Africa are still dominated by agriculture and, therefore, the primary sector. Many of the rapidly developing countries of East and Southeast Asia are dominated by industrialization and, thus, the secondary sector. And services, the tertiary sector, form principal elements of the U.S., European, and Japanese economies.

Not only do countries have different patterns of dominance by each sector, but the dominance of one sector over another may change over time. Until the end of the 1700s all countries were characterized by the primary sector and were principally agricultural. The 1800s saw a few countries emerge with economies characterized by industrialization; first England, then the United States and Germany. The current century has witnessed the emergence of the dominance of the service sector, a characteristic of the most complex modern economies. That the service sector should dominate an economy is a phenomenon that only began to appear in the middle of this century, occurring first in the United States.

It is from this dynamic, in which certain sector activities dominate an economy and change over time, that the perception of an information society has emerged.

In 1962, American economist Fritz Machlup, in his book *The Production and Distribution of Knowledge in the United States*, presented the innovative idea that the U.S. economy could no longer be analyzed solely in terms of mining and agriculture, manufacturing, or services. He concluded that nearly the largest sector, over a fourth of the gross national product, was a "knowledge industry." It consisted of goods and services produced through education, research, and development: information machines and services, and communications.

In the following decade this thesis was further reinforced by another economist, Marc Uri Porat, who proceeded in *The Information Economy* to measure knowledge or information as part of U.S. national income. He concluded that in the twentieth century the information sector had been the most rapidly developing and was emerging as the dominant vehicle of revenue for the American economy.

The information activities of an economy have thus come to be seen as a "fourth sector." The dominance of economies by an information sector has now been observed worldwide. It has come to be viewed as the dominant sector in any more complex or advanced economy.

The work of these two economists established the foundation for the now-accepted perception of societies dominated by information. Popular perception and acceptance of this thesis occurred because something of the phenomenon can be easily observed in daily life. The means for producing and transmitting information, primarily through computers and telecommunications, have massively and globally increased perception of what is produced, information itself. Personal computers, e-mail, and/or fax machines in every office and many homes have reinforced the validity of the original perception of the emerging dominance (even deluge) of information in modern life.

The importance of educational advisers to this modern socioeconomic phenomenon is fundamental. Education is at the heart of the information production process. Not only does education produce information, it reviews it by analyzing, questioning, and reexamining it.

Advisers maintain information on education: where is the best place to study or do research, how to define what is best, and how to be admitted and sustain oneself in the places considered most appropriate. Educational advisers, with their information about education, are essential to maintain the flow and advance of an information society.

Given that this is the role of the educational adviser in modern society, what then is the specific role of the overseas educational adviser, of the adviser for international education? To answer this, let us examine the role of education in another contemporary phenomenon, the internationalization of the globe.

EDUCATION AND GLOBAL INTERNATIONALIZATION

The internationalization of the globe refers both to a process in which parts of the world become more deeply aware of and affected by their interaction with other world areas, and to a policy and practice that move toward further interaction. A host of activities and sustaining structures have comprised the momentum for this interaction, but trade and its ancillary activities of transportation and communication are primary among them.

Economic activities occurring across numerous national boundaries have maximized the quantity and variety of goods and services available around the world. In this context, when a student or scholar goes from his or her own country to another for study or research, it is generally due to the availability of a better or more appropriate service abroad.

Yet there is a very important distinction between international activity in the negotiation of goods and services and international activity for education. International educational exchange is the key resource to sustain the other activities. This point is daily observed by overseas advisers.

How do they observe this truth? Trade around the world of manufactured products, raw materials, and international services builds daily to crescendo volumes. Who largely sustain this? Businessmen, engineers, and computer and high-tech specialists. And what are the areas most sought by foreign students and scholars wanting to study, intern, or do research in the United States? Business administration, engineering, and computer science.

A remarkable example of this integration of international trade and education is displayed in the regions of the former Soviet Union. A momentous event of our history has been the collapse of their state-controlled economies. Anxious to receive investment, to become integrated into world markets, they have given priority to obtaining foreign expertise through study abroad, primarily in the United States or Western Europe, or through foreign universities setting up courses in their countries. Two major exchange programs, the Soros Foundation and the International Research and Exchanges Board (IREX), exist to support this drive, maintaining extensive networks of educational advising offices in Eastern Europe and Russia.

International education is a singular factor in advancing and sustaining global internationalization. It is not just one service among many negotiated around the world; it is the service that allows so many other goods and services to be internationalized.

Education further comprises another key component of internationalization. Continuing the internationalization process requires creating and maintaining an international culture and attitude. Since international education is a cross-cultural experience, it contributes to developing this atmosphere.

Thus, as the resource that produces the trained personnel for continued international activity and as the experience that reinforces a transnational cultural outlook, education is fundamental to global internationalization.

What then is the role of OSEAS and overseas or international education advising in this contemporary historical development? Again, the adviser has information—information on educational opportunities in other countries. The adviser controls an indispensable resource (access to information) and is essential for the flow and advance of internationalization.

International education advising thereby intersects with two vital developments in modern society. Within the development of information and knowledge as dominant activities of modern society, it orients to education, the producer of information and knowledge. Within the process of global internationalization, it orients to the educational opportunities that sustain the process of internationalization and does so with a cross-cultural context that reinforces the process.

Thus, advising as an information service for international education intimately supports two of the most fundamental phenomena of contemporary history. With so momentous a responsibility and opportunity, how has this service developed, and how should it develop?

WHAT HAS BEEN DONE

At the beginning of the last decade, I began to organize the national coordination of overseas educational advising in Brazil. (The first national counseling workshop was held in Rio de Janeiro in 1981; advising was then sometimes referred to as counseling.) I felt that three things had to be done to standardize what was a crucial need for a dependable, professional information service for the public: (1) professionally define and organize advising; (2) provide regular basic and advanced training opportunities for advisers; and (3) supply and maintain adequate materials for advising offices.

It soon became apparent that these standards, achieved through organization, training, and materials, were necessary not just in Brazil but in all of South America, and indeed in all regions of the world. In a remarkably rapid period (less than a decade) these standards began to appear nearly everywhere, albeit unevenly. I believe the rapidity and extent with which they have been applied shows the fundamental relevance of, need for, and interest in advising.

How rapidly and thoroughly has overseas advising been professionally standardized? In terms of organization, the Working Group of U.S. Overseas Educational Advisers in South America, the first regional organization of overseas advisers, was established in 1984. Two years later OSEAS was established within NAFSA and was organized worldwide on a regional basis.

In terms of professional definition, the first directory of advisers for a region (South America) was published by the South American working group in 1984. It was followed by a worldwide directory with approximately 300 entries, published by the College Board Office of International Education. Since the end of the last decade, an OSEAS electronic database has existed, now holding directory information for almost a thousand advisers.

In addition, advising newsletters circulated regionally and worldwide; and in

1987 *The Advising Quarterly* was inaugurated. The following year OSEAS produced its pioneer statement on ethics, "The Overseas Educational Advisers' Code of Ethics."

In terms of training, the United States Information Agency (USIA) began in 1984 to sponsor workshops in the United States for overseas advisers from each region of the world, conducting them at the time of the annual NAFSA conference. In 1987, the College Entrance Examination Board published a revised and significantly enlarged second edition of the *Overseas Educational Adviser's Manual*, even changing the name, substituting adviser for counselor. Moreover, with the establishment of OSEAS, its regional organizations began sponsoring workshops in their respective areas, significantly expanding the possibilities and range of training.

In terms of materials, by the mid-1980s the Minimum Reference Bookshelf (MRB), a basic collection of advising materials, was distributed worldwide by USIA to all advising centers it sponsored (about 300) and was regularly updated. Videotapes and publications for various aspects of orientation to U.S. study multiplied. And most excitingly, in their workshops and newsletters, overseas advisers displayed or recounted details of materials they were producing, from handouts to tape recordings. I recall that in the early 1980s the then-head of the USIA Student Support Services asked me what I believed was most important to develop for advising: book collections, handouts, workshops, videotapes, newsletters. . . . I replied that I thought the most important resource upon which to concentrate would be training, because from trained personnel all other things would flow.

DEFINING ADVISING FOR INTERNATIONAL EDUCATION AS AN INFORMATION PROFESSION

The accumulated activities of the last decade came to identify overseas advising as an "emerging profession." The service of advising was seen to combine or to coalesce around several professions: library service, information center administration, counseling, management, and diplomacy.

Of all these, however, the disciplines which most support and reflect the service of advising are library and information science. Indeed, as previously observed, advising offices very much resemble a category of libraries known as special libraries. They have a collection of specialized resources for a clientele with specific information needs.

Having referred to library and information science, one needs to distinguish among key information professions today: librarian and information scientists, information managers, and computer scientists and telecommunications engineers.

Librarians gather and maintain information resources on deposit for either a general community, such as in a public library, or a specific one, such as in a university, medical, or law library. The information science aspect of librarianship refers to the way in which the library work of gathering, maintaining, and conveying information occurs increasingly, sometimes even primarily, through electronic or computerized means and resources.

Information managers operate within an organization or corporation, gathering and storing data and information, then analyzing and distributing it to the appropriate components of the organization or corporation. Computer scientists and telecommunications engineers are the technological components of the information professions, particularly for development of hardware and software.

Advisers, like librarians, gather and maintain collections of materials for their users' research. They also partially have information management roles, analyzing their resources for the institutions of which they are a part, ensuring that a needed information product is received. Moreover, advisers must be able to use computers and telecommunications in order to efficiently perform their role as conductors of educational information. What remains is for advisers to more fully absorb practices from these established information professionals.

WHAT NEEDS TO BE DONE

I have discussed the very powerful roles of information in modern society and education in the internationalization of the globe, thereby demonstrating the vital role that advising has as an information service. For the information society, educational advising leads one to education, the font or producer of information. For the internationalizing globe, it leads one to international education, the key producer of the personnel and culture for the dynamic of internationalization.

Understanding this historical context, recognizing the relevance of international education advising, and recalling the rapidity and extent with which overseas advising has organized lead to the realization that advising must now advance from the stage of an emerging profession to that of a more systematized and refined one. That refinement must absorb the principles and practices of librarianship, the key information profession for maintaining specialized information. With that accomplishment, educational advising can then serve its information management role for international education.

From library and information science, four areas must be incorporated into the principles and practices of advising: (1) collection development, (2) materials cataloging, (3) reference service, and (4) library and information management.

A knowledge of the techniques of collection development will incorporate into advising an organizational structure for acquiring and maintaining the resources for its services. These techniques include (1) defining the collection of resources, from catalogs and guides, file materials, and alumni contacts to electronic databases and computer networks; (2) locating and maintaining communication with the sources of one's materials, publishers and producers, software and hardware engineers; (3) evaluating one's resources; and (4) maintaining funds for acquisitions.

Cataloging materials organizes resources by classifying them and then storing them so they can be maintained and retrieved as economically and efficiently as possible. In a national library setting, materials are no longer cataloged repeatedly by individual libraries. Once an item is cataloged, it enters a national computer database, thereby avoiding repetition of effort and accelerating access.

Reference service includes the techniques by which information from resources is conveyed. The techniques include the reference interview, by which a librarian responds to a client's need for information. There is also user education, teaching individuals how to use printed, audiovisual, and electronic resources and how to conduct their research.

Library and information management refers to two types of management. Library management concentrates on the management of the library itself, as a unit with its own administrative needs and procedures. Information management focuses on the role of a library within a larger organization or system, having responsibility for gathering and disseminating information in the larger enterprise.

Collection development, cataloging, reference service, and library and information management treat the entire information process, from the gathering of information to its storage or retrieval, its communication, and its maintenance.

Incorporating the principles and practices of these four aspects of library and information science will make advising a much more secure information service and support the development of advising as the information arm of international education.

International education advising, therefore, has a key role in relation to the information age and internationalization of the globe. For the former it gives informational access to education, the key producer of information. For the latter it gives informational access for forming the personnel and culture of internationalization. In less than a decade, overseas advising has rapidly and globally developed its organization, training opportunities, and materials distribution. That emerging profession now needs professional refinement as an information service, adopting library and information science practices of collection development, cataloging, reference service, and library and information management.

The historical context of information in society and of global internationalization, to which educational advising is crucial, have been outlined here, and methods to refine that development suggested. These phenomena are part, nonetheless, of a much larger process—the physical, social, and intellectual evolution of humankind.

In this regard, therefore, it is appropriate to recall the words of the visionary French theologian, Pierre Teilhard de Chardin, who saw so clearly the integration of humanity. This development is an integral part of international education. Let us recall from Teilhard's *The Phenomenon of Man*: "Man is not the center of the universe as once we thought in our simplicity, but something much more wonderful—the arrow pointing the way to the final unification of the world in terms of all life."

2

Gathering Information

The previous chapter concentrated on the character and importance of advising for international education in the contemporary world, highlighting U.S. overseas advising. It urged the development of advising as a professional information service and advocated the application of the principles and practices of library and information science to achieve that objective. The next four chapters will examine how collection development, cataloging, reference service, and library and information management can be applied to advising.

Collection development refers to the acquisition and maintenance of the information resources needed for a particular public. In this chapter, therefore, we will begin by asking what an advising collection is, and what kinds of materials it contains. Giving consideration to every possible kind of material for a collection is fundamental, because only if we are aware of the widest types and amount of materials will we be able to meet the greatest number of demands. Having considered what kinds of materials are in an advising collection, we then want to consider what specific works and titles to include. Finally, we will look at who can provide such material and the techniques for acquiring it. Of course, as previously observed, the focus of materials is for U.S. education.

THINKING OF "THE COLLECTION"

As an overseas adviser, you no doubt have a collection of materials you use in advising your public. Yet when "collection" is referred to, what do you think of as being contained in it? Is it reference books listing colleges that offer certain majors? Is it the catalogs of colleges? How important are these? Are just books the "collection"? What about brochures, handouts, videotapes, or compact discs?

For a moment, however, before continuing with these questions, consider your satisfaction as an adviser and the happiness of an advisee at the moment one of them found just the information for which he or she had been searching. Remember the young high school boy who found an English course that also taught use of computers and was located near his American cousins in Texas. Recall the college girl graduating in economics and wanting to know about admission to a Master of Business Administration (MBA) program, and finding out about that and even more after watching a videotape on the admission process to American graduate schools of business. And think of the junior research physicist with a government grant about to go to the Massachusetts Institute of Technology (MIT) and discovering that there were local physicists who had been to MIT and were willing to give him orientation on the school and its environment.

And do not forget the frustration, the sadness, the bewilderment of those who did not find what they needed. (Of course, there was nothing you could do for the fellow who wanted to study at Harvard and live in California.)

Those people who were satisfied, who obtained crucial information for themselves, did so due to resources which you as an adviser had gathered. For the above cases you were prepared with brochures on English courses, a videotape on graduate business education, and a file of local alumni willing to give orientation. You also probably showed the economics student some business school catalogs and the physics researcher the MIT catalog. You may have had these catalogs available on microfiche or compact disc with copies of pages available by using a reader-printer.

These resources brought the satisfaction. They comprised a considerable spectrum of materials, from brochures and videotapes to an alumni file along with college catalogs in paper, microfiche, or compact disc form. For other cases (or these same cases at a later date) you would have offered other resources: reference books, an audiocassette tape, or a computer database. Your advising and the satisfaction of you and your advisees, therefore, depended on the availability of wide resources to meet a variety of needs.

Advisers' thoughts about their collections of advising materials, about the books, catalogs, brochures, handouts, files, videos, audiotapes, compact discs, computers, and more are as fundamental as an irrigation engineer thinking about water or a banker thinking about money. In each case, they are thinking about the substance, the very nature, of their work.

For advising, the collection of materials is fundamental to the advising operation. Without it there is no operation; there is no advising. What is in the collection, how much, how good, how it is organized, and how accessible are fundamental issues an adviser must always consider.

The collection, therefore, is not just something ancillary to advising, something "on the side." It is not just a shelf of books along the edges of the advising center. The collection is the whole breadth of resources an adviser uses and teaches advisees to use. Information resources and their use are the substance, the nature, of advising. Thinking about the "collection" is thinking about your advising and how much it will be able to do.

A good mind-stretching exercise for advisers is to list how many different kinds of materials make up an advising collection, comprise the ways of providing information. The length of the list may just turn out to be the size of advisee satisfaction. In making this list, you are really trying to determine the full extent of your resources, the amount and variety of tools you use to carry out advising.

1. Books may be the first things on the list. But what kind of books? There are reference books, such as *The Official Guide to MBA Programs*, the annual directories from Peterson's Guides, or Gale's directory of research centers. These are specialized works for educational opportunities in the United States. There are also reference works, such as dictionaries and style manuals, that an advisee may use in preparing study plans.

Other books are college and university catalogs. These too are of different types. There are general catalogs of universities and specialized ones for certain schools or colleges, such as engineering, music, or nursing.

These publications may not be in paper format only. Certain guides are available as computer programs or on compact discs, and catalogs are available in this format and on microfiche. Thus nonprint materials are part of the collection. Moreover, the readers or reader-printers to use these formats integrate the collection as support for it.

2. Periodicals for advising, though limited, consist of *The Advising Quarterly*, *Lovejoy's Guidance Digest*, the *NAFSA Newsletter*, and newsletters produced by some regional OSEAS organizations. They are valuable in advising because of the current information they carry on new or special fields of study, for reporting on new or revised government regulations affecting foreign students, or describing the programs of local advising workshops.

3. Brochures and pamphlets comprise a significant part of an advising collection. They are produced by English-teaching courses, high school exchange programs, departments and schools of colleges and universities, financing agencies, and so on. How one stores them can be as varied as they are: in boxes, folders, albums, or filing cabinets.

4. Handouts or general information sheets are further resources in a collection. These deal with explaining the American undergraduate or graduate educational system, English proficiency courses, high school exchange programs, or financial aid opportunities and are prepared locally by an advising center.

5. A "contacts" file is a collection of the names of persons in your community or the United States who can be highly useful to advisees. This file consists of cards giving information about individuals who have returned from study in the United States (alumni), of local educational personnel and government officials, and of American professors and educational personnel an adviser has met in the United States or who have visited locally. The cards indicate individuals' backgrounds and how they can help advisees and advisers. They

can be interfiled with cards that list these individuals by their academic specialization and/or institutional affiliation. One thus has groups of local consultants by discipline and by institution. The alumni in the file can also participate in orientation programs sponsored by the advising center. An example of some cards from a contacts file can be seen in Figure 2.1.

Such a file will probably take up the least amount of space in your office, but can be among your most effective resources. The direct contact it allows, permitting you to clear up an admissions bottleneck for an advisee, clarify a bureaucratic obstacle in a government procedure, or get more background on a financial aid possibility are all examples of its usefulness. I inherited such a file from my predecessor at the advising office in Rio de Janeiro, and I continued it for the rich resource it always provided. Such a file, of course, can easily be made into a computer database with keyword searching benefits.

6. Video (along with audio) tapes often play a large part in the various stages of informing an advisee about education in the United States. Videotapes explaining the admissions process, costs, reference sources for researching schools, the visa process, and life in an American school may comprise the initial stage of advising. Such tapes may exist for undergraduate or graduate education. They can also be used in predeparture orientation, the last stage of advising, to show something of life in the United States. Tapes are also available for specific schools, frequently for recruitment purposes.

If videotapes or the equipment to run them is too expensive for an advising office to purchase, audiocassette tapes and a player may be more economical and accessible. Moreover, slides or filmstrips may substitute video.

7. Electronic and computer resources are a growing part of advising operations and will have more and more of a role. Peterson's graduate study guide is available on compact disc. Keeping track of advisees' progress in their research can be done with a computer database. Certain college catalogs can be consulted via e-mail. E-mail also provides communication networks for advisers, such as OSEASNet, whereby they can consult among themselves regarding advising cases, a book acquisition, or other matters.

Electronic resources are and will be growing as much in advising centers as they are throughout all libraries and information services. It is quite conceivable that one day they will dominate advising. One can imagine an advising "console booth" of the future, an enclosed desk with a computer, large monitor, and printer, at which some future advisee might sit. Advisees would begin by activating a videodisc describing the procedures for admission to the type and level of education they seek. On request they could receive printouts of information sheets as the program proceeded. They could read reference books and catalogs via full-text retrieval. Having selected several schools to consider, these advisees of the not-too-distant future could examine them in videodisc tours. Interactive options would allow listening to sample lectures at schools under consideration, or examining their libraries, laboratories, or foreign student advising office. Further, such advisees will be able to complete and return their applications electronically.

8. You. Me. Us. We are the greatest resources of our collections. No one knows better what all the other resources are or can do. We do not sit on shelves or lie in files like the others, but we are surrounded by them. We are in the center of them—quite literally possibly, depending on individual office floor plans. We and our advising colleagues are the table of contents and index to everything in the collection.

In making this list, I hope I may have surprised you with something that was included. Possibly you had not thought of a contacts card file or audiocassette tapes as part of an advising collection. But these are resources, and the idea of this exercise has been to help you realize that your collection is all your resources. The ultimate objective, of course, is to realize that all your resources represent the capacity you have for doing effective advising. Given this ultimate end, thinking about your collection is thinking about the potential and substance of your advising.

I hope I may have left something(s) out of the above list and that you discover it—or them. It will show how much you have stretched in this exercise.

Advisers in one-person advising centers may be thinking that it is impossible for them to acquire all such materials. Yet remember that the above is not a mold; it is a stretching exercise. Most of the advising centers around the world do not have all of the above kinds of materials. Moreover, several of the most useful items above can be self-produced, such as the contacts file or the audiotapes. More expensive items, such as a computer, compact disc reader, or printer should always be on a "wish list," with all the details of an order prepared. When an administrator in your organization comes around asking for new equipment needs, you will be ready. Of course, you should have already begun demonstrating your needs to this individual.

FINDING OUT WHAT IS NEEDED IN A COLLECTION

Having thought about the extent and variety of items making up a collection, we now want to consider what is specifically needed in it and how to go about identifying such needs. Needs are of two kinds: items which are basic requirements of a collection and those which are particularly wanted by different interests. Whether you are building a new advising collection or maintaining an older one, determining basic or general along with changing or special needs is a continuing function of responding to your advisees.

Guides

Collection development guides exist for numerous types of libraries, and advising is no exception. In this respect, therefore, a classic work is Joanne Abed's *The Library that AMIDEAST Built*, published by the America-Mideast Educa-

Figure 2.1
Contacts File

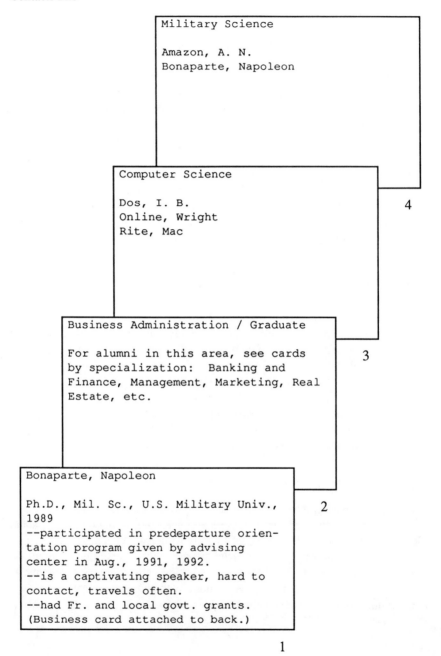

Military Science

Amazon, A. N.
Bonaparte, Napoleon

4

Computer Science

Dos, I. B.
Online, Wright
Rite, Mac

3

Business Administration / Graduate

For alumni in this area, see cards
by specialization: Banking and
Finance, Management, Marketing, Real
Estate, etc.

2

Bonaparte, Napoleon

Ph.D., Mil. Sc., U.S. Military Univ.,
1989
--participated in predeparture orientation program given by advising
center in Aug., 1991, 1992.
--is a captivating speaker, hard to
contact, travels often.
--had Fr. and local govt. grants.
(Business card attached to back.)

1

Figure 2.1 (continued)

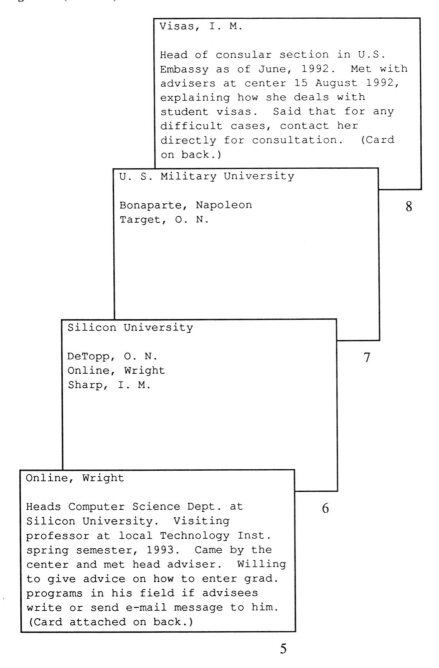

```
Visas, I. M.

Head of consular section in U.S.
Embassy as of June, 1992.  Met with
advisers at center 15 August 1992,
explaining how she deals with
student visas.  Said that for any
difficult cases, contact her
directly for consultation.  (Card
on back.)
```

```
U. S. Military University

Bonaparte, Napoleon                        8
Target, O. N.
```

```
Silicon University

DeTopp, O. N.                          7
Online, Wright
Sharp, I. M.
```

```
Online, Wright

Heads Computer Science Dept. at        6
Silicon University.  Visiting
professor at local Technology Inst.
spring semester, 1993.  Came by the
center and met head adviser.  Willing
to give advice on how to enter grad.
programs in his field if advisees
write or send e-mail message to him.
(Card attached on back.)
```

5

Cards for contacts can be interfiled with ones for
contacts' specialization and institution, allowing group
identification of them by discipline or affiliation.
This file can be made into a computer database.

tional and Training Services (AMIDEAST) in 1985. It is a concise work (thirty pages) that lists the books and other printed materials the author acquired to meet the needs of the AMIDEAST office in Washington, D.C.

The library of AMIDEAST serves as a resource center for the advising offices of AMIDEAST throughout North Africa and the Middle East. In this respect, the work outlines the collection of a small research library for educational advising. It is not itself an advising office, and therefore its collection does not extend into all the resources previously cited (the tapes, handouts, files, etc.) needed in day-to-day advising. *The Library that AMIDEAST Built*, therefore, serves as a guide to building a solid book section for an advising center.

Moreover, since it was published in 1985, many new publications have appeared. As a supplement to this work, there is the 1992 *Guide to Educational Advising Resources* from AMIDEAST, compiled by Juleann S. Fallgatter, Lia G. Hutton, and Jane A. Conklin. This guide is an annotated bibliography of all the works that might be useful in an advising library by levels and types of study in the United States. Not every advising center will necessarily want to have all the works listed in it, but all centers will be interested in knowing how they can find what they do want.

The *Guide to Educational Advising Resources* lists over five hundred titles, giving a brief description of each book or pamphlet and including the publisher's address, phone, and fax numbers, together with the price of the work. It is seventy-seven pages long and consists mostly of guides by fields of study. Thus its opening section describes guides for study in accounting, acoustics, and advertising, and it goes on to design, medicine, watchmaking, and writing. Covering well more than a hundred fields of study, it is an exceptionally rich resource for study in the United States in just about every field of human knowledge or endeavor. Of the many interesting works it describes, among the most beneficial are its listing of the surprising number of publications which can be acquired free of charge. In addition to the principal section of the book on fields of study in higher education, it also includes sections on guides to primary and secondary education, technical schools and junior colleges, home study, undergraduate and graduate study, financial costs and aid, internships, and return-country readaptation. (A revised edition is forthcoming.)

Since both of these works come from AMIDEAST, you may be thinking that it would be an interesting library to visit when you are in the United States. AMIDEAST is located at 1100 17th Street, N.W. in Washington, D.C. 20036–4601. Its phone number is 202–785–0022 and fax is 202–822–6563. (Since it is not open to the public, making an appointment for such a visit is important.)

Another office you might want to visit if in the United States is the advising center of the Institute of International Education (IIE). This is the only "overseas" educational advising center actually in the United States. It functions as an information center for Americans wishing to study abroad and for foreigners in the United States wishing to study in this country. Its library presents not only an excellent book collection but also videotapes, handouts, brochures, and more—all the numerous resources of a well-stocked advising office. It is located in front of the United Nations at 809 U.N. Plaza, New York, NY 10017–3580. The phone number is 212–984–5418, and the fax is 212–984–5452. Despite the great number of users, this center depends almost exclusively on volunteer advisers, so it is thus also a good example of such advising.

Another source of information for building an advising collection, important from a number of perspectives, is the *Bibliography of Suggested Reference and Orientation Materials for Educational Advising Centers* from USIA. The 1993 edition of this work describes the thirty-three items that comprise the minimum collection for advising for the previously cited MRB, and a truncated, bare-essentials version of this, the Select Reference Collection (SRC). Appendix A of this book lists the titles included in these collections. They are automatically received by advising centers which the U.S. Information Service (USIS) post-designates. (USIS is the cultural and public affairs section of U.S. embassies and consulates. They are coordinated by USIA in Washington, D.C.)

The USIA bibliography includes sections describing works which can supplement the basic collections. It includes references not only to books and pamphlets, like the AMIDEAST works, but also to periodicals. This work is important, therefore, both for its hierarchy of focus from basic to more advanced collections and for its wide variety of print materials. Furthermore, it is useful because it is frequently updated. Unfortunately, it is not a work one can simply order from a publisher. It is distributed to USIS-supported advising centers, meaning those at American cultural centers, USIS posts, or Fulbright Commissions. An adviser outside this network will benefit from consulting it but must request it from one of these centers.

Outside books, pamphlets, and periodicals, information about handouts, audiovisual, and electronic resources are not quite as plentiful. One source, although partial, is the previously mentioned *Overseas Educational Advisers' Manual*. This work, as its title indicates, is primarily a training manual for advisers. Nonetheless, it has sections with instructions for making handouts, accompanied by models; some recommendations regarding video titles and instructions for producing videos; and a discussion of computer uses (although from the perspective of 1987, when it was published). Actually, for electronic resources and computer applications in advising, the best indications currently come from recent (since 1990) issues of *The Advising Quarterly*.

For film and video useful in advising, a very good source is *Film and Video Resources for International Educational Exchange* by Lee Zeigler. It has numerous titles of use for topics and activities in advising centers, such as orientation to college and university study in the United States, living in this country, English courses, high school exchange programs, foreign teaching assistants, and readaptation. Of further usefulness is its information on distributors of film and video. This work will be complemented shortly by a new publication which NAFSA is preparing, a guide to nonprint materials for advising.

From the above sources for collection development, an adviser obtains indications of specific items for the kinds of materials needed in advising. But the information is weighted to print over nonprint materials, and it is somewhat scattered and not always easily accessible. What is critically and urgently needed now in overseas educational advising is a current bibliography or collection development guide which includes all materials, print, audiovisual, and electronic, available for advising.

We have been discussing what is needed in an advising collection. So far I have indicated works which show what is available for standard needs. However, how does one go about identifying the particular needs of advisees in your center? Moreover, what methods can you use to ensure that you are keeping up with their changing needs?

Surveying User Needs

There are several ways in which libraries and many other services survey the needs of their users. One of the most traditional is by questionnaire. Increasingly, another method is the focus group. Both of these methods can be highly useful; however, they meet different objectives for identifying user needs.

Before considering these two methods, the objectives for conducting a survey should be examined. In *The Book of Survey Techniques*, Joseph M. Viladas emphasizes several points about surveying. You should be able to state precisely the purpose of the survey. Precisely identifying purpose(s) beforehand is important for refining questions asked. Such preparation is worthwhile because a well-conducted survey will indicate materials users find wanting in the collection and those which are adequate or strong; can strengthen budget requests; and can reveal staff strengths and weaknesses.

Another consideration to make in preparation for a survey is the relevance the information will have for the decisions you have to make. If you suspect that you must increase staff and your survey identifies that the public also feels staff is wanting, you will have to decide about hiring someone. Who will you hire based on the information you obtain? Someone at a professional salary level or paraprofessional? Is staff lacking at certain times of day or of the week so that a part-time person might be satisfactory? Could volunteers be used? These questions will determine the kinds of questions you ask and the applicability of the information you obtain.

Finally, before conducting a survey, you want to consider several things about it. How much time will be necessary to organize it? To carry it out? To evaluate it? These considerations are important in order to avoid becoming involved in a project that takes more time than it is worth. Thinking at this stage may allow you to reformulate either how important the information you seek really is or how the survey can be more focused and reduced.

You must also think in terms of the advisees who participate in the survey. How much time do they want to give to completing a form or participating in a discussion? The time required from them may be the crucial factor deciding whether they will or will not participate. The purpose of surveying is to have information that will result in action. You do not want a survey that interferes with you or others acting.

Figure 2.2 offers an example of one way of conducting a survey—the questionnaire. Note how it carries out several of the points made about surveying. It is focused on one problem, trying to find out about the adequacy of advising materials. This focus, however, has two considerations. One is the adequacy of the materials themselves; the other is relating adequacy to knowledge of how to use materials.

The questionnaire is also designed to be easy to complete and to evaluate. It is only one page. Half the questions need only a simple check mark or yes-no response. Those respondents wishing to make extended comments are given such an opportunity on the reverse side of the page. In gathering data from this questionnaire, the adviser should only have to give attention to extended phrasing in question number four; number six may also have a long answer; number eight definitely will if it is answered.

A focused and convenient questionnaire allows more of them to be completed and evaluated, widening the data and information from which you can make decisions. Yet no matter how careful one is in preparing questionnaires, invariably there is a question interpreted in two or more ways. or which asks something that is ambiguous or puzzling to the respondent.

Practice with questionnaires, accumulating experience about what questions were effective or ineffective, further aids in improving one's expertise in their production. Knowing the principles of surveying beforehand saves much time in acquiring the technique of their composition. Further assistance in preparing them is available in *Questionnaires: Design and Use* by Douglas R. Berdie et al.

The advantage of questionnaires is that they can produce objective, tabulated information. However, if an adviser wishes to obtain more qualitative information (that is, personal opinions and reactions of advisees), one should consider organizing a focus group. In addition to such qualitative responses, the focus group also has the advantage of producing spontaneous opinions and answers one may not have thought about for survey questions.

Focus groups, as the name implies, have a concentrated objective for their discussion because one is trying to obtain focused information on a particular topic in a limited amount of time. One would not have a focus group on the adequacy of, say, all the material in an advising center. Rather, one would concentrate only on those for undergraduate study, English language programs, graduate engineering study, and so on.

In organizing a focus group discussion, an adviser may ask six to ten advisees pursuing information in a particular area or level of study to meet for sixty to ninety minutes to discuss some aspect of that research. As the moderator of a focus group, the adviser has to get a discussion going and keep it flowing, but

Figure 2.2
User Survey Questionnaire

Educational Advising Center
Survey of Adequacy of Advising Materials

So that we might serve you better at this advising center, would you please answer the following questions regarding the adequacy of our materials.

1. What have you been researching at this center for study in the United States?

2. How many times have you been here to research?

3. Please give a rating from 1 (lowest) to 10 (highest) of the materials you have used here. Please do not give a rating for materials you have not used.

____ Books   ____ Handouts

____ Pamphlets and Brochures   ____ Microfiche

____ Videotapes   ____ Audiocassettes

____ Computerized resources

4. If you found any of the above materials inadequate, what was wrong with them?

5. Are there any materials here that you think you do not adequately know how to use?

____ Yes ____ No

6. If yes, what are they?

7. Have staff been helpful for you in understanding how to use materials?

____ Yes ____ No

8. For further comments, please use reverse side.

Thank you for helping us with this survey.

not dominate it. Such dominance defeats the purpose of the meeting—getting opinions from users of the advising center.

An effective way to begin a focus group (after introductions) is to restate the purpose of the meeting and then allow each participant to react and elaborate upon that. One participant may begin to speak about using certain books, understanding a handout or videotape, or dealing with American university application forms. Others are thereby stimulated to further respond and elaborate. This exchange and dynamic produce the variety and unexpected information a questionnaire does not capture.

In the United States it is customary to make an audio, even a video, recording of focus group discussions. People in some other cultures may not feel comfortable about this method, but certainly they will understand the adviser-moderator taking notes since gathering information is the purpose of the meeting.

The Viladas book gives further ideas for organizing focus groups. Moreover, the article by Richard Widdows et al. in *College and Research Libraries* (July 1991), "The Focus Group Interview: A Method for Assessing Users' Evaluation of Library Service," explains the application of focus group methods to user evaluation of libraries.

Out of experience with group discussions of the advising collection, an adviser might consider establishing an advising collection advisory board. Virtually all libraries have such boards or councils. In large libraries these bodies are composed internally, bringing together the heads of collection divisions and some sections in order to coordinate development of the collection as a whole.

For an advising center such a board could consist of characteristic types of users. Members could be both present and past advisees. However, for stability of composition, the board might have to have a good many users who have returned (that is, alumni, not those who are going). The board should also have someone who represents the organization of the advising center, such as an officer of the binational center, Fulbright Commission, or USIS post. This member can then be more attentive to meeting the financial requirements for collection needs. If the adviser is not a librarian, the board might also have a librarian member or some other information specialist to further support the professional development of the collection.

One way of composing this board would be suggesting a list of candidates to the person responsible for supervising the advising center within the organization to which the center belongs. This person would then make the invitation to join the board. The adviser and this supervisor would be ex-officio members. How often the board meets, quarterly or semiannually, and how long members serve and the board renewed, can be determined either by the board itself or the adviser together with the supervisor. Of course, given the extensive variety of how advising centers operate within other organizations, the hierarchy of supervising individuals involved in the above process can vary greatly.

If hesitant about having such a board because it may come to interfere in the operations of the advising center, an adviser can consider calling it on a one-time or occasional basis, like an ad hoc committee and similar to the focus groups. One thus obtains the benefit of the guidance without the onus of interference. Another ad hoc committee which could significantly benefit a center where the adviser is not a librarian is one of a selected team of librarians acting as volunteer consultants.

Peers

Besides consulting guides and users, another way of identifying and satisfying user needs is through consultation with advising colleagues. For most professionals, peer consultation occurs relatively easily and routinely: doctors and nurses with their colleagues in hospitals, teachers in their schools, engineers in their offices and on projects. These groups also have regular or national conferences, journals, and newsletters.

Such ease and frequency of communication is rare for overseas advisers scattered in their small numbers around the globe. National or regional conferences occur irregularly. Under the best circumstances they are biannual. Newsletters too are sporadic. Recognizing the importance of peer consultation for the crucial objective of identifying and satisfying user needs, this is all the more reason for advisers to demand frequent and regular conferences.

An immediate though limited solution which is emerging for the problem of inadequate peer consultation among advisers is e-mail networks. Since 1992, OSEASNet, an electronic communication network for overseas advisers, has existed. It is accessed by sending a message to: eried+@osu.edu. There are more than a hundred advisers on this network in more than several dozen countries. It brings together over 10 percent of the advisers registered in the directories of the OSEAS database. Regional electronic networks are also emerging, such as OSEAS-EUROPE, for advisers in Europe, accessed by sending a message to Hopkins@csc.fi.

These networks circulate information on new books available for advising, discuss ethical issues, respond to requests for information in advising cases, discuss preparation for meetings or conferences, and many other topics. For a small segment of advisers, electronic networks are a singular advance in allowing them to somewhat reduce the barrier of isolation from peers. These networks are a strong reason for all advisers to obtain e-mail; but they are no substitute for the direct communication and interaction of regular conferences. Advisers must continue to advocate for conferences—indeed, such discussion has been a heated topic of OSEASNet.

Collection Development Policy

Once a library identifies materials for its collection through guides and identifies needs through user surveys, it then must implement collection development through policy and acquisitions. The collection development policy is the plan of the library for building and maintaining its collection and a statement to staff and users of this plan. A collection policy for an advising center is the highest professional expression by which an adviser publicizes a plan for the advising collection, resulting from extensive consultation of guides, users, and peers.

A collection development policy statement accompanies the mission and goals statement of a center (the latter to be discussed in Chapter 5, dealing with management). Both understand that one has identified who one's public is.

A mission and goals statement and a collection development policy respond to fundamental questions. Who is your advising public? Whom do you advise? How and with what do you advise? Some advising centers respond only to inquiries on study in higher education, for undergraduate or graduate study. Others respond to a full spectrum of study from preschool and elementary education to secondary education and high school exchange programs through English, technical, and short courses on to college, university, and postdoctoral study. Moreover, they answer information needs on financial aid, visas, predeparture orientation, and return-country readaptation. In addition to this information directed for study or research in the United States, some centers also advise both American students and those of other nationalities about study and research in the country of the center. The advising boundaries of the center must be clearly defined in a mission and goals statement before a collection development policy can be determined. Of course, this policy will change as the parameters of the advising center's mission may.

Figure 2.3 is a sample collection development policy statement. Notice that it is quite brief and emphasizes two points: what types of materials are collected and for what purpose. If an advising center publishes a brochure explaining its activities, such a statement could easily be the main text of the publication. Although brief, nonetheless, as an information professional you know the time put into the background of its production. It is a product of the environment from which it emerged, of thinking of the collection in terms of the center's mission, user needs, and expertise from guides and peers regarding resources to meet needs. One of its fundamental qualities is that it incorporates change as part of its policy.

A great advantage of having the statement is in regard to responding to change. Suppose a policy of expanded diplomatic relations occurs between the country of the advising center and the United States. To effect this new policy, it is decided that there should be more high school exchange opportunities between the two countries.

A new type of information, on secondary education, will be needed in the center. Moreover, it will have to focus on both the United States and the other country. Different kinds of orientation and readaptation programs will have to be designed and conducted.

The center may prove very willing to adapt its mission to the change. However, the collection statement will demonstrate quite specifically that, to do

Figure 2.3
Collection Development Policy Statement

```
              Educational  Advising  Center
            Collection Development Policy Statement

The collection of the Educational Advising Center consists
of books, pamphlets, periodicals, and handouts together with
audiovisual and electronic resources.  These materials are
primarily in the English language except for some of those
of an initial orientation nature, which are in the language
of this country.  In general, materials are of a reference
nature and, therefore, for use only in the Center.

The collection covers, in accord with the mission and goals
statement of the center, the following types and levels of
material for study or research in the United States.  All
materials are as current and ample as possible.
        --Undergraduate study for degree programs
        --Graduate study for degree or certificate programs
        --Postdoctoral study or research
        --English courses related to preparation for a course
          in higher education
        --Financial aid for higher education
        --Predeparture orientation and return-country
          readaptation

This policy is subject to change as modifications may occur
in the mission and goals of the Center.
```

more, additional funding will have to be given to the center. If advising of a
certain type was done with one budget, then an additional service requiring
more books, handouts, audiovisual resources, and adviser time will cost pro-
portionately more.

The policy statement is also helpful in situations in which a person is dissat-
isfied with the center because it fails to offer certain information. Someone may
complain that a center, such as that represented in Figure 2.3, does not have
information on all-girl, private high schools in the United States. When the
adviser receives this complaint, presenting the collection statement shows that
the deficiency is not due to some arbitrary manner of acquiring materials but to
the planned parameters of the collection. However, if more such complaints are
received, it is time to consider changes in the mission of the center and, thereby,
its collection policy.

Developing Public Library Collections, Policies, and Procedures, written by
Kay Ann Cassell and Elizabeth Futas for small and medium-sized libraries,
is a useful work to consult should you wish to know more about collection
development. This work is one in a series for self-help librarianship entitled

How-to-Do-It Manuals for Libraries, produced by Neal-Schuman, a specialist publisher for libraries.

Weeding

Generally one associates libraries with acquiring materials, and we have seen the array of practices which determine this fundamental activity. However, there are a number of reasons why a library or advising center must systematically weed or discard from the collection.

Materials that are out of date can become misinformation, the exact opposite objective of an information service. Moreover, heavy use of materials may have made them deteriorate. Interest in a certain field of study may have passed, but its materials continue occupying space. There may be duplicate copies of materials. Thus the factors determining what to weed are essentially time (something is out of date) or use (something is no longer used or has seen more use than it can bear).

Weeding can be done on a continual and/or systematic basis. In the process of advising alone one will encounter works in a collection meeting the above conditions and remove them. Nonetheless, weeding should also occur on a scheduled basis so that items not seen during advising routines are also examined. Since many advising materials are published on an annual basis (college catalogs and many guides), once a year is a good recommendation for weeding. It can be done very conveniently at the same time one conducts inventory.

How does one dispose of weeded materials? Discarding does not immediately mean throwing away. Indeed, given the effort that many advisers put into obtaining materials, they might feel they are getting rid of a part of themselves.

As a rule, with items still having at least some use, one wants to pass on to others as many weeded materials as possible and to give them where they will be used the most. Duplicate items can be given to other advising centers. You may also consider sending items to the library or study abroad information center of a university in your city. There may also be a guidance counseling office at a local American school which could use materials.

After disposing of weeded items to where they will be used most advantageously, an adviser can give consideration to some items (like multiple duplicates of a book or pamphlet on American education) that might be considered as gifts for individuals who have participated in focus groups or a collection advisory committee.

Items that are too worn or outdated may be considered for an annual used book sale by the center. Used book sales, like flea markets, are an example of how one person's trash can be another's treasure. Such a sale might be the source of income for acquiring several new books. What items remain after the sale will finally have to go into the trash.

KNOWING ABOUT AND OBTAINING
ADVISING MATERIALS

Having determined what is needed in an advising collection, advisers must then know the sources and techniques for acquisition. Knowing from whom you can acquire materials can be done by setting up two information systems: an automatic reception system, in which you are regularly informed about who is producing what, and a structured pursuit system, in which you routinely examine certain sources of information to find producers.

Automatic Reception of Publishing Information

There are a number of publishers and associations from whom you will regularly want to receive catalogs or lists of publications. With a form letter (see Figure 2.4) costing little more than the postage and time to complete it, you can place your advising center on the mailing list of dozens of publishers and organizations which will automatically inform you of their latest book and non-print materials. Who are some of these entities, and what is the value of their publications?

First group. It consists of publishers who specialize in producing books which are guides (print as well as electronic) to programs or types of study in American colleges and universities. They may also publish works with information of a support nature for such study. These publishers and their addresses are:

Barron's Educational Series
Order Department
250 Wireless Boulevard
Hauppauge, NY 11788

It publishes guides not only for college admission but also business and law schools, together with preparation for examinations such as The Test of English as a Foreign Language (TOEFL) and the Scholastic Assessment Test (SAT).

The College Board (also College Entrance Examination Board)
Publications Department
45 Columbus Avenue
New York, NY 10023–6992

The College Board produces not only *The College Handbook* and *Index of Majors* (with a foreign student supplement) but also books on college costs and transferring within colleges. It also produces numerous software programs for finding and selecting college programs, calculating costs, and acquiring financial aid. Furthermore, it offers videotapes on the admission process to colleges. Moreover, as the producer of the SAT, it has numerous types of preparation works for this exam. As we have seen, it also is the publisher of a fundamental

Figure 2.4
Form Letter for Requests

```
          Educational  Advising  Center
               123  Education  Road
               98765  Cityville
                    Country  X
     Phone  Number    Fax  Number    E-mail  Address


Date


        Blank area for
        address of recipient.


Greetings:

Would you please send this office:




        Blank area for item(s) being requested.




Sincerely,



O. N. DeJobb,
Educational Adviser
```

If your advising center is able to use the APO, include a paragraph in this letter giving such an address and the fact that it allows mail to be sent at U.S. domestic postal rates.

work in advising, the *Overseas Educational Adviser's Manual*. Moreover, the International Education Office of the College Board in Washington, D.C., a crucial support for advising, prepares the *Directory of Overseas Educational Advising Centers* (USIA-affiliated).

> Lovejoy's College Guides, Inc.
> P.O. Box Q
> Red Bank, NJ 07701

Lovejoy includes not only a college guide (which includes a section on American colleges abroad) but also extensive exam preparation, application, admission, and financial aid publications.

Macmillan Publishing Company
866 Third Avenue
New York, NY 10022

Unlike other publishers in this group, Macmillan does not devote most of its publishing to college guides and admission materials. Nevertheless, it publishes one of the oldest college guides, *The College Blue Book*, available in print and on compact disc, and also has works on extension or correspondence education.

Peterson's Guides, Inc.
202 Carnegie Center
P.O. Box 2123
Princeton, NJ 08543–2123

Peterson's Guides has not only its annual directories of undergraduate and graduate study, but also books regarding the most competitive colleges, schools for the disabled, nondegree certificate programs, internships, electronic and correspondence education, athletic scholarships, grants for graduate study, and technical schools. Peterson's *Gradline* is its annual guide to graduate study on compact disc.

Advisees seek not only guide or directory types of publications but also orientation as to the best places at which to study. *Educational Rankings Annual* is a yearly compendium of rankings and lists in education gathered from education and general interest publications. (It is published by Gale Research, Inc., whose address is given later in this chapter.)

Another annual evaluation publication is the issue of *U.S. News and World Report* appearing at the beginning of the American academic year, focusing on the best colleges in the country. It ranks not only the major research universities, or national universities, but also national and regional liberal arts colleges, and large and small comprehensive colleges. The survey for the article is conducted using a number of objective statistical factors together with subjective ones based on the opinions of university administrators. This weekly news magazine is generally available in the libraries of American cultural centers abroad. Requests for this special issue can be sent to:

U.S. News and World Report
Order Division
2400 N Street, N.W.
Washington, DC 20037

A further source of regular information on rankings is published in the *Gourman Reports*. These reports are controversial since they do not include complete information on the methodology or sources for their compilations. The *Gourman Reports* are distributed by:

Dearborn Trade
520 N. Dearborn Street
Chicago, IL 60601–4354

To get a balanced perspective on ranking and assessment publications, including some of the above, you can consult "Ranking Colleges and Universities," by Jennifer Chambers, in the Spring 1990 issue of *The Advising Quarterly*. Further, "Concepts of Quality and Ranking" by Joanne Abed, published in the *Overseas Educational Adviser's Manual*, includes an annotated bibliography citing numerous other works on the subject.

I am not as critical of ranking information as some. In my advising experience I have rarely found that a school listed as "very good" academically was not that. The deficiency which occurs in these rankings is that they can overlook good places. I find rankings not so much inaccurate but incomplete. Moreover, these rankings primarily deal with "best" in terms of academic distinction. However, what is best in this regard is not necessarily best for every individual. Some advisers may prefer not to receive the publications catalogs of these publishers or order their works. Nevertheless, a very significant part of questions from advisees, virtually as high as those on financial aid, will be about the quality of study programs. Pointing out which are accredited will hardly be a sufficient response.

A second group of publishers. It includes those who produce works of a background or support nature for study in American higher education.

American Council on Education (ACE)
One Dupont Circle
Washington, DC 20036

ACE publishes a key annual work, *Accredited Institutions of Post-secondary Education*, along with background works on U.S. education, such as the *International Visitor's Guide to U.S. Higher Education*.

American Association of Community and Junior Colleges (AACJC)
1 Dupont Circle, N.W., Suite 410
Washington, DC 20036–1176

Council of Graduate Schools (CGS)
1 Dupont Circle, N.W., Suite 430
Washington, DC 20036–1176

It is useful to be on the mailing lists of the AACJC and CGS, in addition to ACE, in order to get the full spectrum of publishing information on higher education from junior colleges to graduate study.

Educational Testing Service (ETS)
Order Section
P.O. Box 6108
Princeton, NJ 08541–6108

The most important items one receives from ETS are the registration bulletins for its exams, TOEFL, the Graduate Record Examination (GRE), and the Graduate Management Admissions Test (GMAT). As aids to taking these tests, it publishes books, audio tape kits, and software programs for exam preparation. Moreover, it publishes a guide to graduate programs, the *ETS/CGS Directory of Graduate Programs*, similar to ones by the publishers in the first group.

American College Testing Program
2201 North Dodge Street
Iowa City, IA 52243

Another college entrance exam publisher is the American College Testing Program. It produces the American College Test (ACT) and materials ancillary to it.

Arco Books
200 Old Tappan Road
Old Tappan, NJ 07675

Arco publishes an extensive series of books for preparing college admissions exams and the application procedure.

Educational Commission for Foreign Medical Graduates (ECFMG)
3624 Market Street
Philadelphia, PA 19104

Commission on Graduates of Foreign Nursing Schools (CGFNS)
3600 Market Street, Suite 400
Philadelphia, PA 19104

Test registration bulletins for foreign doctors and nurses are published, respectively, by the ECFMG and CGFNS. They also send to those on their mailing lists for these bulletins information about changes in testing regulations.

Gale Research, Inc.
835 Penobscot Building
Detroit, MI 48226–4094

Gale Research is a major American publisher of reference works. Among its many publications, the two most important for educational advisers are the *Encyclopedia of Associations* and the *Research Centers Directory*. These works are of great usefulness in finding sources of information for study or research in very specialized or obscure fields.

Higher Education Publications, Inc.
6400 Arlington Boulevard, Suite 648
Falls Church, VA 22042

This publisher is important for its directory of U.S. higher education and its compendium of costs for undergraduate education.

NTC Publishing Group (formerly National Textbook Company)
4255 West Touhy Avenue
Lincolnwood, IL 60646–1975

NTC has a wide range of publications, among which are practical guides designed for foreign students seeking admission to American colleges and universities.

There are also several sources which publish important financial aid information for American higher education.

Foundation Center
79 Fifth Avenue
New York, NY 10003–3076

National Science Foundation (NSF)
Publications Department
1800 G Street, N.W., Suite 232
Washington, DC 20550

Oryx Press
4041 North Central Avenue, Suite 700
Phoenix, AZ 85012–3397

The Foundation Center publishes numerous titles related to grant giving by American foundations. Among some of its works are the *Foundation Grants Directory* and *Foundation Grants to Individuals*.

The NSF has publications on preparing grant requests, financial aid, and the quite significant role of foreign researchers in U.S. science and technology. As a cost control measure, the NSF makes many of its publications available electronically. They can be accessed through the Science and Technology Information System (STIS) of the NSF. To do so send an e-mail message to: stisserv@nsf.gov. In the body of the message, write ''get index'' to receive a list of NSF documents available for electronic retrieval.

The Oryx Press publishes the *Directory of Research Grants* together with specialized grant directories for the humanities, biomedical, and health fields. It also offers electronic grant searching capability through *OnDisc*. Moreover, it publishes numerous works on applying for grants and has many background titles on American higher education. It produces the annual *Accredited Institutions of Higher Education*.

A third group. It consists of organizations and publishers involved in international and cross-cultural education.

AMIDEAST
1100 17th Street, N.W., Suite 300
Washington, DC 20036

AMIDEAST is the publisher of *The Advising Quarterly,* the professional periodical for advisers, and of books on resources for advising (mentioned earlier).

Council on International Educational Exchange (CIEE)
205 East 42nd Street
New York, NY 10017

One of the most important activities of CIEE is the discount travel service it offers students. As a publisher, it concentrates on educational opportunities abroad for American students, which foreign students in the United States can also take advantage of. Besides the reduced fare travel opportunities it offers U.S. or foreign students, it also provides publications specifically for student visitors from abroad, such as *Where to Stay USA* and a guide to volunteer service in the United States.

Impact Publications
9104-N Manassas Drive
Manassas Park, VA 22111–5211

Somewhat like IIE, Impact is primarily a publisher of works for Americans about opportunities for travel, work, or study abroad. However, it has some works of interest to foreign students, such as its *Guide to College Programs in Hospitality and Tourism.* For a U.S. study abroad adviser or a multinational adviser in a European university, this publisher is a prime source of information on numerous and varied international opportunities.

IIE (address previously given) is a main source of publications on statistics, such as *Open Doors* and *Profiles*, and policy regarding foreign students in the United States together with financial aid, *Funding for U.S. Study*. It publishes *English Language and Orientation Programs*, a guide to English language courses in the United States. It is a major publisher of works for Americans on study abroad or other international experiences, somewhat like Impact Publications.

> Intercultural Press
> P.O. Box 700
> Yarmouth, ME 04096

Intercultural Press is notable for its books on adaptation to other cultures. Among some of its many titles are *American Ways: A Guide for Foreigners*, *The Exchange Student Survival Kit*, *The Handbook of Foreign Student Advising*, and *Living in the U.S.A.*

> NAFSA: Association of International Educators
> 1875 Connecticut Avenue, N.W., Suite 1000
> Washington, DC 20009–5728

Knowing of NAFSA's publications is of central importance for advisers. It publishes works as wide-ranging as the *Adviser's Manual of Federal Regulations Affecting Foreign Students and Scholars* to *Foreign Teaching Assistants in U.S. Universities* and *Optimizing Health for Foreign Students in the U.S.* In addition, it produces a number of videotapes for adaptation to American academic and cultural life. OSEAS is part of this organization, so key publications on advising originate through NAFSA.

> UNIPUB, Inc.
> 4611-F Assembly Drive
> Lanham, MD 20706–4391

UNIPUB is notable for its books in comparative and international education and for background on international business and economics, particularly in a European context.

Fourth group. A difficult, yet highly important group of publishers, comprises academic and professional associations who publish guides to undergraduate and/or graduate study in their discipline or profession. The great usefulness of these guides is that they give descriptions of all the departments or schools in a particular discipline or profession. They often include specialization indexes, thereby offering a key source for finding more refined or obscure topics of study or research. The range of fields to which an adviser must respond and have a book budget for will determine how many of the publication catalogs or lists from these organizations to receive. The following is a selection of some associations and their respective publications for advising, showing a sample of who constitutes this publishing group.

American Society for Engineering Education
11 Dupont Circle, Suite 200
Washington, DC 20036

It annually publishes *Engineering College Research and Graduate Study*. Engineering is one of the most sought-after fields for study in the United States. This title is of prime importance, along with anything else of a related nature that this engineering education society publishes.

American Medical Association (AMA)
Circulation Department
P.O. Box 10946
Chicago, IL 60610–0946

The AMA publishes an annual, *Graduate Medical Education Programs*, and the *Allied Health Education Directory*. Again, one of the most sought-after fields of study in the United States is medicine.

Economics Institute
University of Colorado
Publications Center
1030 13th Street
Boulder, CO 80302

This institute publishes the *Guide to Graduate Studies in Economics and Agricultural Economics: United States of America and Canada*.

National Association of Schools of Art and Design
11250 Roger Bacon Drive, No. 21
Reston, VA 22090

This association publishes *Directory: National Association of Schools of Art and Design*.

University Aviation Association
3410 Skyway Drive
Opelika, AL 36801

University Aviation Association publishes the *Collegiate Aviation Directory*. As you can see, listing the publishers in this group would be as lengthy as the diversity of organizations representing the fields of study or professions in which humankind endeavors. In addition to the above associations and their publications, the National Dance Association, the American Geological Institute, the American Chemical Society, the National Association of Schools of Music, the National League for Nursing, the American Association of Dental Schools, and each of their study guides in their respective disciplines could be mentioned, along with many others. Yet even indicating all of them, one would still not have all of the publications originating from these sources.

It is hence not possible to list here all these associations and their publications. That would be another book. Indeed, it is a book already (previously mentioned), the *Guide to Educational Advising Resources.* Acquiring this book is an excellent way to see what is available from these specialized publishers for the advising information sought. Out of these many sources, you can then determine on whose mailing list it is most important for you to appear.

Fifth group. The final group of publishers and entities about whose works an adviser should be regularly informed is those who produce guides or directories for study in primary or secondary education and for technical and vocational education.

Educational Directories, Inc.
P.O. Box 199
Mount Prospect, IL 60056

Educational Directories publishes *Patterson's Elementary Education, Patterson's Schools Classified,* and *Patterson's American Education.* The latter lists the addresses and often phone numbers of public and parochial school administrators in the United States. In addition, it has a section on technical and trade schools.

Career College Association (CCA)
750 1st Street, N.E., Suite 900
Washington, DC 20002

National Home Study Council (NHSC)
1601 18th Street, N.W., Suite 2
Washington, DC 20009

The CCA (formerly the National Association of Trade and Technical Schools) has as its principal publication the annual *Directory of Private Accredited Career Colleges and Schools.* The NHSC publishes the annual *Directory of Accredited Home Study Schools.* From both of these organizations one receives useful information and developments in vocational and correspondence study.

Porter Sargent Publishers
11 Beacon Street
Boston, MA 02108

The last publisher in this final group, Porter Sargent, publishes the *Handbook of Private Schools* and the *Guide to Summer Camps and Summer Schools.*

The above system will bring you numerous publishers' catalogs you will want to have. Nonetheless, titles can still be missed. Such missed works come from major publishers who only occasionally produce books relevant to the above groups. Such is the situation, for example, of St. Martin's Press producing *Insider's Guide to the Colleges.* However, you could add this press (175 Fifth Avenue; New York, NY 10010) to the second group of publishers, if only to know when new editions of this title might come out.

In order not to miss publication information which does not come to you automatically from publishers, you can set up a system whereby you regularly review sources of information on new advising materials.

Structured Pursuit of Publication Information

Structured pursuit means regularly reviewing certain periodical literature to find new advising materials. The following publications (with publisher address) are recommended for this objective.

The Chronicle of Higher Education
Circulation Department
1255 23rd Street, N.W.
Washington, DC 20037

The Chronicle is a weekly newspaper of higher education in the United States. It has a regular section, "New Books on Higher Education," which concentrates on new works giving background information on higher education in the United States, and sometimes includes materials relevant to advising, such as guides or directories (do not confuse this section of *The Chronicle* with another, "New Scholarly Books"). In addition, it regularly covers news in international education. Since this newspaper will have a limited readership in your advising center, possibly only you and any other professional staff in your center, you may economize on its subscription by checking whether the local American cultural center library in your community receives it. If it does not subscribe, do not hesitate to request that it make such a subscription for the usefulness it will have to you and many others interested in U.S. higher education. Here you have a chance to express a "user's need."

Choice
100 Riverview Center
Middletown, CT 06457–3445

This monthly magazine is one of the most concise and comprehensive reviews of new literature for college and university libraries. "Literature" means not only new books but also periodicals and audiovisual or electronic resources. It covers all disciplines, giving a summary and evaluation of each work. The sections of *Choice* most important for advisers are those on reference and education. Its reviews are noted for their cogency and authority, allowing efficient evaluation of new publishing in all academic fields. All reviews are done by university teaching faculty who are specialists in the fields of the works being evaluated. If you do not want to subscribe, again see if your local USIS or American cultural center library receives it or will subscribe to it. (Note: As the network coordinator for OSEASNet, I make digests of relevant advising items from *Choice* and circulate them on the network. Here is another reason for getting e-mail and becoming a member of OSEASNet.)

The Advising Quarterly (for address, see AMIDEAST) is the professional periodical for overseas advisers. A subscription is a professional must for advisers. It is a source of information on new publications for advising through its book reviews and in its section on fields of study.

Lovejoy's Guidance Digest (for address, see Lovejoy's) is a monthly review which is highly useful for following developments of new majors or special fields of study in American colleges. It also has practical advice in relation to college application and admission procedures together with campus living.

Book reviews in the *NAFSA Newsletter* (for address, see NAFSA) only rarely cover items which are tools for educational advising. Its reviews are more useful as sources of information on American and international education. (Note: I do a column, "Riedinger Reviews," for this publication, which is a digest of new books and articles in international education. Its usefulness to advisers is primarily as background material.)

Another way of checking new materials is through the annual publication *Books in Print*, from R. R. Bowker. This multivolume work allows one to find almost all available books in print in the United States. The current set (1994) comes in ten volumes—not something an advising office can easily afford to order. The first three volumes are for searching books in print by author; the next three, by title; and the next three, by subject. The last volume lists publishers, including their addresses and phone numbers. This is such a standard library working tool that an adviser should be able to find it at any American library abroad.

It is the subject volumes of *BIP* (the abbreviation by which *Books in Print* is usually referred to) that are most useful for checking new publications. These volumes have, for example, subject headings for all disciplines and professions. These are subdivided for (among many things) vocational guidance and examinations. Thus, one finds headings such as "Economics—Vocational Guidance" and "Engineering—Vocational Guidance." Under these are listed all books in print which are guides to study in these fields.

Another sample set of subject headings is "Economics—Examinations, Questions, etc." and "Engineering—Examinations, Questions, etc." This section indicates books available for preparation in exams, from school admission to professional licensing.

Other subject headings list works for correspondence courses, English as a foreign language, foreign students, student aid, research grants, and more. As you can see, this can be quite an efficient way of checking for all materials available for advising. It allows you to find things that "get through the cracks" in your system of being informed through publishers' lists or by reading periodical literature. You will be amazed in consulting *BIP* at some of the treasures that got by you. A drawback to *BIP*, however, is that one uses this source a year or so after new publications may have come out. It is available on compact disc. *BIP* also includes a section listing the name, address, and communication numbers for most publishers in the United States. Bowker also publishes *Forthcoming Books*, indicating new books to be published over the next several months, which has a subject section. (For foreign *BIP*s, see page 132.)

Should you wish to know more about some of the titles you find, you can examine them in a compendium of publishers catalogs called the *Publishers' Trade List Annual* (*PTLA*), another Bowker publication and universal American library tool. This work brings together in a multivolume set the catalogs or lists of many (although not all) publishers. Even though you will see these catalogs or lists later than if you received them directly, with this work there is a way of examining titles from many dozens of publishers. Incidentally, as you may have suspected, R. R. Bowker is a publisher which specializes in American publishing. It is the agency in the United States which issues the International Standard Book Number (ISBN), the worldwide system for numerically identifying titles and editions of books published in each country. No doubt you would also be interested to know that it happens to be the publisher of the *Annual Register of Grants*.

R. R. Bowker
121 Chanlon Road
New Providence, NJ 07974

Another work to examine is the *Guide to Reference Books* and its supplements, published by the American Library Association (ALA). This work divides reference books first by field of knowledge or human endeavor and then divides within these fields by type of reference work (that is, dictionaries, directories, encyclopedias, guides, handbooks, etc.). The section on foundations and philanthropic organizations yields many useful handbooks (for example, *Foundation Fundamentals: A Guide for Grantseekers* by Carol Kurzig). In the sections on business, economics, sociology, and so on, the subdivision for directories lists such books for places in which to study in these and numerous other fields.

American Library Association (ALA)
50 East Huron Street
Chicago, IL 60611

To know about new compact discs, you will want to consult the annual publication *CD-ROMS in Print International* (Westport, Conn.: Mecklermedia). The subject index for this work includes sections for "directories" and "education and training." Moreover, there is a section giving the name, address, and communication numbers of manufacturers around the world.

For information on periodicals, you can consult *Ulrich's International Periodicals Directory*, a Bowker publication which lists periodicals by subject. It includes contact information for the publisher of each periodical.

A final way of keeping informed about new advising materials is through your contact in USIS, the cultural section of the local American consulate or embassy. USIA, the parent organization, not only distributes books, pamphlets, and videotapes but also contracts for production of such materials. Further, it provides training opportunities in the United States for overseas advisers. Maintaining contact with USIS ensures that such information is passed on to you, the adviser.

If you want to keep abreast of current research and publishing on foreign students in the United States or on international education, you can consult the *Current Index of Journals in Education* and *Resources in Education*, published by the Educational Resources Information Center (ERIC). Abroad you are most likely to encounter these publications in the libraries of schools or colleges of education, and possibly in some of the larger American cultural center libraries. ERIC acquires and stores both standard journal and research material together with items that escape standard collection development practices. Educational advisers should be aware of this policy. If they publish newsletters, do reports on the conditions of advising in their countries, or on national or regional advising workshops, they should send copies of such materials to ERIC for indexing and storage. Copies of the materials are made available upon request by researchers at cost. The contributions of materials by overseas advisers can greatly aid in bringing the activities of international advising to the attention of researchers in international education. Advisers can send their materials to:

Acquisitions Department
ERIC Processing and Reference Facility
1301 Piccard Drive, Suite 300
Rockville, MD 20850–4305

The Mechanics of Ordering Materials for Advising

Ordering materials from a publisher is a simple procedure. One can either complete a catalog ordering form or send a form letter similar to Figure 2.4. In requesting by letter, one should specify, besides a title, a catalog number or ISBN (or, for periodicals, an International Standard Serial Number [ISSN]), to avoid confusion about what one is ordering. A photocopy of the order should become part of one's ordering file. Shipping, handling, and overseas postage generally add an average of 10 percent to the cost of an order. Moreover, for orders sent outside the United States, prepayment is usually required in the form of a check, draft, or money order in U.S. dollars. Having a business credit card can eliminate much of this international payment paperwork. If an order is not received within forty-five to sixty days, the process of claiming should begin, requesting clarification as to why an order has not been fulfilled.

It is rare nowadays for libraries to order books or other materials from publishers. To economize time, most libraries order through a book vendor. This is a company which stocks and/or orders publications on a large scale. Libraries contract with these vendors to send automatically all the types of materials they want. A library writes a plan of acquisitions for the vendor as guidelines regarding the materials to be sent. These guidelines are known as subject profiles, and consist of detailed instructions to a vendor of what to send.

Vendor plans come in various types, but that most appropriate to an advising center as a small library would be a "gathering" or "blanket order" plan. In such a plan, the company gathers and sends everything within the library's subject profile for a determined period of time. The library makes a deposit with the vendor for the estimated cost of these materials, which are being ordered in a wide or blanket fashion. In this way the librarian is freed from the book ordering process and concentrates on supervising the vendor plan to see that it is sending what is being published. If the wrong types of books are sent or the right ones missed, the vendor must be advised, the profile made clearer, or, ultimately, a new vendor found.

Figure 2.5 is an example of a gathering or blanket order plan with a vendor, together with its subject profile. Advisers should consider the convenience of such a plan for their ordering. Notice in the model plan how it follows the collection policy statement in Figure 2.3. Indeed, for a vendor to better understand an advising center's needs, the collection development policy statement should be sent together with a subject profile. For each type of material requested, the plan specifies examples of titles and publishers. Observe that there is a potential problem in this plan, to which the adviser monitoring it is going to have to pay attention. The request for specialized guides to fields of study requires that the vendor deal with noncommercial publishers with whom the agent is not familiar. Actually, the adviser who follows what is being newly published may know more than the vendor, accustomed to dealing with commercial publishers. The adviser can help the vendor by alerting this agency regarding what the adviser has recently come to know about new publications. An adviser can also send requests for materials not in the subject profile to the vendor, using the vendor for all book or periodical requests rather than writing individually to each publisher. Vendors, however, may take more time to fulfill orders, having to acquire for themselves what they do not have in stock.

Logistically, it is more convenient to have a plan with a book vendor in one's own country. Locally, therefore, bookdealers who import American and English-language materials should be contacted about the possibility of such a plan. If you are not familiar with these dealers, you can inquire with a large university or public library that deals with such vendors.

If a local vendor is not possible, an American one may be considered. While there are many library vendors in the United States, they are accustomed to dealing with large-budget plans in the range of thousands of dollars. The following have expressed interest in hearing about plans for advising materials.

The Book House, Inc.
208 West Chicago Street
Jonesville, MI 49250

Yankee Book Peddler, Inc.
999 Maple Street
Contocook, NH 03229

The Book House can respond to a traditional gathering plan. If you wish to inquire about such a plan, send a draft of a gathering plan (using the model) with your first inquiry.

The Yankee Book Peddler offers a much less traditional and quite innovative type of vendor plan, one by e-mail. It allows one to receive electronically a registration form indicating the kinds of books one wants to be notified about when they are published. Regularly after such registration, a client receives an e-mail alert of publications in one's profile and then can send an electronic request to order them. One also indicates the type of shipping preferred (surface or air mail, an international delivery service, rush delivery, etc.). Payment is by credit card, another reason for an advising center to have a business credit card—not to mention e-mail. For information on joining this plan, called LibroLine, send an e-mail (telnet) message to: libro@office.ybp.com.

If you wish other options for buying materials on a vendor plan or as single orders, you can find stores specializing in education and reference books in another Bowker publication, the *American Book Trade Directory*. In making a first inquiry with a vendor, be sure to indicate the conditions for mailing or shipping to your country. To know more about vendor plans, you will want to consult *Managing Acquisitions and Vendor Relations* by Heather S. Miller. This is another in the Neal-Schuman series of library how-to-do-it manuals mentioned earlier.

Figure 2.5
Gathering or Blanket Order Vendor Plan with Subject Profile

Educational Advising Center

1. The following is an agreement between this Educational Advising
Center (EAC) and the Universal Bookdealer Company, Inc. (UBC) to
establish a gathering plan for the former based on the following subject
profile. The value of this plan is in the amount of US$1,000 (one
thousand U.S. dollars) and extends from 1 January to 31 December 1994
with the option of renewal.
2. Send the following types of books published in the years 1993 and
1994 (only 1994 for those works published annually):

   A. Guides or directories listing and/or describing courses in
American colleges and universities. These publications should include
works such as the Peterson's annual guides, The College Handbook and
Index of Majors and works of a similar nature from publishers such as
Barron's, Lovejoy's, and MacMillan's.

   B. Guides or directories for specific disciplines such as the
Official Guide to MBA Programs from Random House. Materials from non-
commercial publishers should also be sent such as Graduate Study in
Psychology and Associated Fields from the American Psychological
Association or the Directory of Geoscience Departments from the American
Geological Institute.

   C. Guides or directories which focus on special conditions in
American colleges or universities for minorities or women.

   D. Guides to sources of financial aid, such as athletic
scholarships or federal grants, and manuals on how to apply for such
aid. Do no send materials which apply only to American citizens or
permanent residents.

   E. Works related to adapting to American culture, particularly
any dealing with the academic environment.

   F. Inform EAC, but do not send, any of the above items which
become available in electronic formats.
3. EAC will deposit $1,000 with UBC no later than 30 days after the
starting date of this plan to cover the cost of books, other materials,
and their shipment. Each shipment of books must be accompanied by an
invoice together with a statement of the balance of the account. EAC
does not have the right to reject books under this plan. However, if
the above subject profile is not satisfactorily followed, this plan may
not be renewed after its ending date.
4. Shipments are to be sent by international air post. UBC will send
materials in good condition. It is not responsible for damage during
shipping.
5. A copy of the collection development policy statement of EAC
accompanies this plan in order to further clarify EAC collection
interests.

A City
The Date

Figure 2.6
Order Record Card

```
 ╭─────────╮      Guide to Financial Aid for College, 45th
│ Location │      ed., 1994
│ Code     │
│ Space    │
 ╰─────────╯


Ordered:   22 Feb 94

Arr:

Notes:  --Letter from publisher 23 Mar 94 saying book sold
out.  Will inform of new printing.
--Note from publisher 20 May 94 saying second printing
being done.  Will send order.
```

This card can serve as a record both for orders and the
collection catalog. As an order record it indicates when an
item was ordered and arrived together with notes regarding
the order. Once the order arrives and the work is placed in
the collection, the card can be transferred to the
collection catalog, seen in Figure 3.3. There is a space in
the upper left hand corner to indicate its location in the
collection.

A vendor plan is already in operation for some overseas advising centers.
The materials which USIA sends to the advising centers it supports with the
MRB and SRC can be considered beneficiaries of a gathering plan (see Appendix A for titles included in the MRB and SRC). USIA acts as a gatherer of key
advising materials and sends these to the several hundred advising centers it
supports around the world. The ''vendor'' aspect of this plan does not operate
because these advising centers do not have to pay for the materials.

The MRB has been functioning for almost a decade and has been a singular
contribution to standardizing overseas advising materials worldwide. But as its
title emphasizes, it is a minimum or basic standard. It is the core of an advising
collection. Around it much other collection development and ordering, as outlined here, has to be done.

Records must be kept of orders made either to a vendor or publisher. Figure
2.6 is an example of an order card. Notice that it identifies the book by title
only. Many advising materials do not have individual authors. Title, therefore,
is the one element of an advising item that makes it a universal access point for
all records. Notice that the card also has space for indicating when an item was
ordered and received. As soon as the order does arrive, this card can go from
your order file to the collection catalog. (Such a transfer is suggested in order

to save the time of writing two cards. The library procedure would be to have two—which you can follow if you prefer and have the time.) The upper left hand corner of this card has been left blank for placing its location in the collection. The upper right hand corner is not used, to avoid smudging as users go through the catalog. Records such as these are also excellent candidates for a computer database.

Printed Materials from Colleges and Universities

A large and significant part of an advising collection consists of general catalogs from colleges and universities. There are also specialized catalogs, such as those from business, education, library, music, or nursing schools within a university. Moreover, departments within schools produce materials such as brochures from finance or marketing departments within business schools and from chemical, civil, or electric engineering departments within schools of engineering. Catalogs change each academic year.

This material is of the utmost importance to advisees, who obtain from it detailed information regarding program contents and admission requirements. However, the process of acquiring it can be among the most time-consuming and vexing in advising. No advising center has all the general, specialized, and departmental information these institutions print. There is no centralized system for acquiring this material. As a result, each adviser around the globe orders these catalogs separately and individually.

The difficulties in acquiring this material have several causes. There are over 3,000 colleges and universities in the United States. Trying to order materials from such a multitude of institutions is a quite complicated process. While some universities send general and specialized catalogs together from one request, others require a separate request for the general and each specialized catalog. Even the general catalog may be divided, one for undergraduate and another for graduate study, each having to be requested from separate administrative divisions in the university. Material from departments must always be requested directly from them.

Other complications occur because some universities send catalogs free of charge while others charge for them. Some universities send their catalogs automatically each year once an initial request has been made; others require a new request each year.

The catalogs of more than 3,000 American institutions of higher education are available in microfiche or on compact disc from:

Career Guidance Foundation
8090 Engineer Road
San Diego, CA 92111–1988

A reader is necessary to use these fiche or compact discs, and ideally should be accompanied by a printer. Using such a collection by an advisee is dependent on how many readers are available. Usually an advising office can only afford one. Some advisees do not like using microfiche or compact disc readers because of eyestrain, or mainly because, unlike paper catalogs, they are more cumbersome for comparison back and forth among volumes.

Some universities are beginning to make their catalogs available electronically on the Internet, a U.S. government-sponsored worldwide network of electronic networks. To use these catalogs, however, requires that an advising center or an advisee have a computer which can access these sources.

Ultimately, in regard to ordering catalogs, advisers must decide between balancing catalog availability and user needs against what they can order and maintain in the collection. A microfiche or compact disc collection may primarily serve to make up the difference between the paper supply of catalogs available in a collection and what an advisee may need outside that supply.

Advisers have to decide the proportion (perhaps no more than 10 percent) of catalogs they will be able to collect in relation to user needs. On the whole, an adviser will want at least the general and specialized catalogs of the most-sought or top-ranked three or four dozen public and private universities, as many liberal arts colleges, and the major community colleges.

Ordering college catalogs can be done using the same multipurpose request form letter in Figure 2.4. For general and specialized catalogs, the letter must be addressed to the admissions office of the university or individual school. In a few cases, a request must go to the university bookstore. For departmental material, one writes directly to the departments since they do not have admission offices. Requests should be made at the beginning of the academic year (late August or early September) for the catalogs of that year. Timing of requests is important because if you write too early, you may receive last year's catalog; if you write too late, the supply may be gone.

Keeping a card or computer database record of these requests is important both for your acquisitions control and your collection catalog. Notes on these records will remind you from whom you have to order by request each year and who is charging (and at what rate) for catalogs.

Besides college catalogs, the brochures and pamphlets for English language courses may have to be ordered at least annually and in bulk. Some language schools regularly send bulk shipments of their brochures; others do not, and their brochures need to be requested. This is especially true if you want these materials to represent as many locales in the United States or specialization of courses (that is, English for business, computer, or other purposes) as possible. The addresses of almost all English courses can be found in the IIE publication *English Language and Orientation Programs* (cited earlier).

Equipment and Supplies for Advising Centers

We have examined library practices for knowing about and acquiring publications. Advising centers also need equipment and supplies, much of which can be acquired from vendors of library equipment and supplies. Ideally you will want to acquire such items locally. However, if such companies or their equipment and supplies are limited, you can order from companies in this country.

There are several large traditional library equipment and supply companies in the United States.

Bro-Dart
1609 Memorial Drive
Williamsport, PA 17705

Demco Library Supplies
4810 Forest Run Road
Madison, WI 53704

Gaylord Brothers, Inc.
P.O. Box 4901
Syracuse, NY 13221

You may request their catalogs, perusal of which will give you many ideas for computer furniture, book shelves or pamphlet racks, filing devices, audiovisual equipment, and much more.

Orders for such equipment should have a card or computer database record similar to book and other materials requests. When these equipment orders arrive, the order record passes to an inventory file of all office equipment.

Making One's Own Advising Materials

Invariably there are items that overseas advisers must produce on their own. A standard example would seem to be handouts, especially ones outlining how to be admitted to an American undergraduate or graduate degree program. Such outlines usually need to be written in the local language. (Not knowing English should not be the basis for not being informed about how to study in the United States. Being well informed of the process in one's own language can be a motive for studying English more resolutely.) In addition, as mentioned earlier, these handouts need to include information on how local secondary or undergraduate education fits into preparation for American higher education. Such handouts also indicate what kinds of local financial aid are available or how personal finances in local currency are transferred to American schools in checks, drafts, or deposits in U.S. currency.

What other handouts should one have, and how does one go about making them? It is generally time to make a handout when the following frequency of questioning occurs. If during a week you receive several requests for the same type of information on, for example, how to select and enter an English course or a high school exchange program, then you may suspect a handout is needed.

If these weekly requests repeat themselves over several months, then it is certainly time to prepare a handout for such advisees.

To compose the points of the handout, note what questions occurred repeatedly and what answers were given. Recall also what questions were not asked or what problems were not known and required being mentioned and elaborated upon. For example, few know that financial aid is usually not available for English courses or that there may be local representatives of English courses and high school exchange programs, facilitating selection and admission.

Once all the standard questions and answers are organized into the sequence in which they need to be explained, a draft of the handout can be written. Advisers can use this draft for a temporary period to test how it helps advisees. The final draft can be elaborated and the new handout completed from the comments they provide regarding what is obscure or insufficient information.

A further item that advisers can produce is audiotape cassettes. One use of them is to accompany certain handouts. Because an adviser may not have time to verbally go over the basic procedures in a handout for selecting an English course or high school exchange program, an audio recording of the handout can be made by the adviser. An advisee can listen to this recording, have a copy of the handout, and then consult with the adviser after listening to the recording about points not understood or about aspects of study particular to his or her situation.

Another type of audio recording can be made for various types or stages of advisee research. For example, advisees are usually not familiar with using American college catalogs. A recording can be made explaining what catalogs contain, how they are organized, and what to expect from them. In this manner, every advisee who needs to know this information is given a complete explanation; but adviser time does not have to be used to give each explanation, which may not always be as complete as the recording. Just as handouts are photocopied or reproduced for many advisees, so also an adviser's routine consultations can be recorded and reproduced.

There may also be types of publications needed, besides handouts, peculiar to one's country or region, that an adviser can produce. I advised in Brazil, a country in the Southern Hemisphere. Because of this location, seasons were reversed. Winter was in July; summer vacation went from December to February. (Preferred Christmas trees were the metallic type, which shimmered and glistened not from snow but sunlight. One went to parties not bundled up but tanned.) During "summer break," Brazilians would seek English or short-term study courses in the United States. To respond to this need, my staff and I produced a guide to "courses in the United States during Southern Hemisphere summer." The research for this guide meant a lot of sustained calendar coordination research, but eventually it had quite a surprising number of pages of information. It was distributed to other countries in South America below the equator through a cooperative regional advising organization, established by the advisers in the area, known as the Working Group of U.S. Overseas Educational Advisers in South America.

We have examined the first stage of the information cycle: gathering information. We did so by seeing how practices of library collection development are applicable to overseas educational advising.

This chapter began by emphasizing the fundamental role of the advising collection in allowing an adviser to respond to an advisee. It then detailed the array of materials possible for an advising center and the mechanics for knowing about and obtaining them. Now we will examine how to organize resources so that they can be thoroughly and efficiently retrieved for and by an advisee.

3

Organizing Information

In the previous chapter we concentrated on developing the collection of an advising center. We discussed what types of materials comprise a collection. We were as all-inclusive of materials as possible in order to have the greatest number of resources available for the widest number of inquiries. From types of materials for the collection, we went to considerations of how to determine what specific works and titles were needed. Finally, we examined the sources for providing materials and the procedures for acquiring them.

Now we want to consider how to retrieve materials. We must know how to put in order a considerable amount of advising material so that advisers and advisees have paths of access to retrieve what they need. Therefore, let us examine the concepts and techniques of cataloging, especially classification and filing, and how these practices are carried out and maintained.

Cataloging in a library refers to the process whereby an item, such as a book, periodical, videotape, or other type of item is described and a record of it made as a unique element in the collection. This process is comparable to photographing an item in a museum for identity. In the catalog description, standard pieces of information are always included as the basis for being able to retrieve the item. Continuing the museum comparison, each photo carries a caption indicating what the item is, where it comes from, and from what period.

Library cataloging is done by specialized librarians known as catalogers. They have extensive knowledge of rules, and experience in applying them. Because of the expertise required and consequent time consumed in cataloging, one must recognize that advisers cannot, and indeed need not, become catalogers. Advisers need only know what basically occurs in cataloging and out of that what is applicable and practicable in an advising center for retrieving its materials.

Therefore, in this chapter we will look first at the process in a library for cataloging and then at what (from that process) is most conveniently and efficiently appropriate for an advising center. Advisers, of course, will ultimately decide how much of the formal library cataloging process they wish to use in their centers. This decision will depend on the needs and size of their centers and the availability of time.

In discussing the cataloging of materials in an advising center, I am assuming an advising collection of average size. This would mean several hundred reference books (the guide and directory material previously described), some on compact disc; less than a thousand paper catalogs together with a microfiche or compact disc college catalog collection and an appropriate reader; several hundred brochures and pamphlets; and some video or audiotapes with the equipment to use them. Also assumed is a physical situation and policy that allows users open access to materials. Moreover, there is also a policy to support advisees to become self-reliant pursuers of information.

LIBRARY CATALOGING

Access Points for Retrieval

Libraries organize materials for retrieval in terms of three access points: author, title, and subject. An author may be individual or corporate, and is defined as the one who is intellectually responsible for a work. The Career Guidance Foundation is an example of a corporate author, producer of the collection of college catalogs in microfiche or on compact disc.

Concerning the topic under which a work is categorized, subject access, a work often has more than one such entry. The *Peterson's Annual Guide to Undergraduate Study* includes both U.S. and Canadian schools. There are, therefore, two subject entries for it—one for U.S. college and university directories and another for Canadian college and university directories.

Figure 3.1 shows an example of how one work is entered on records for access by author, title, and subject(s). A user thus can find a work by the name of the author, the title of the book, or under a subject to which it is related. The author card is considered the main entry, and all subject classification information is noted on it. All entries lead one to the basic author and title information.

A key element in each record is the classification number, found in the upper left hand part of all the records. This number precisely classifies the work in terms of subject and type and becomes a means of physically locating the work in the whole collection.

The numbering or classifying of a book (and all other library materials) is based on a system, used in the United States and many other countries, called the Dewey Decimal Classification (DDC) system. This system is considered especially appropriate for small libraries. It is in contrast to the other major library classification system, that of the Library of Congress. The latter system predominates in large research libraries.

The Dewey system is based on numbers in which digits to the left or right of the decimal point have a standardized significance in terms of subject and type. The further digits move to the right, the more precisely a work is described. With this system, items are shelved in a library in numerical sequence and found on the same basis. The tables in Figure 3.2 give an idea of the system's basic operation. It allows access to a work either by author, title, or subject. Once one has found a work by any of these points, one can locate the book by the classification number.

The call number for the book in this example is 378.1056. From previous examination of the Dewey system we know that 3 indicates a work in the social sciences. Within the 300's classification, the next number, 7, is for education; 8 is for higher education. Advancing to the right of the decimal point, the 1 and 0 refer to admission to colleges and universities, the 5 and 6 to guides and examinations. The numbering to precisely classify this book by subject and type has taken us from the general category of the social sciences and then progressed more specifically to education, higher education, admission to colleges and universities, and then guides and exams for such admission.

To make this book distinct from others that are also college entrance guides, the first three letters of the author's surname have been placed under the Dewey number. If there are other guides with the same 378.1056 number, this book will be distinct from them due to its author letters. It will also be located among the 378.1056 group alphabetically by the surname.

Besides the DDC system there is also the Universal Decimal Classification (UDC) system. It is a worldwide adaptation of the original, American-based DDC. I am emphasizing DDC since in this guide primarily American educational materials are being considered.

Library organization of materials gives great attention to organizing by subject matter. This emphasis is due to the fact that the principal objective of most library users when searching is to find information on a certain topic, that is, by subject.

The call number gives the precise location of a book within a subject. Another way in which a library orients readers to their topics of interest is through subject headings on the collection catalog cards. While the call number gives a precise indication of the subject and type of book, the subject heading gives a slightly more general categorization for an item so that a user can find related books on a topic in the same location.

Subject headings in library records follow a regulated language and have a controlled vocabulary. This regulation allows standardization of access in any library a reader might use. The phrasing of subject headings is based on principles of categorizing from the general to the specific, much as the Dewey system. The rules for writing subject headings and the listing of them is done

Figure 3.1
Catalog Cards with All Access Points

Title Card

```
Getting into the top 100
colleges

378.1056            Ranking, Morris
RAN

Getting into the top 100
colleges.
New York:   E-Z In School Press,
1993.   338 pp.
```

Author Card (Main Entry)

```
378.1056          Ranking, Morris
RAN

Getting into the top 100
colleges.
New York:   E-Z In School Press,
1993.   338 pp.
1. Colleges and Universites--
United States--Directories.
2. College and Universities--
United States--Entrance
Requirements.
```

by the Library of Congress. This "list" is currently three (quite thick) volumes long.

An abbreviated guide to subject headings for small libraries is the *Sears List of Subject Headings* by Minnie Earl Sears, a standard tool in American libraries. Should advisers wish to write standardized subject headings for their materials, they should consult *Sears*.

Advisers who have access to the Internet can actually take advantage of what libraries refer to as "copy cataloging." The Internet includes the library catalogs of many dozens of American university and public libraries. One can see how a book has been cataloged in one of these libraries, copying the standardized subject headings it has applied and the DDC call number. The catalogs of both university and public libraries are on the Internet. The former, because of their size, tend to use the Library of Congress classification system. One is more likely to find DDC by accessing the catalog of a public library.

Incidentally, one need not feel uncomfortable about doing copy cataloging. Given the expense and time required for original cataloging, major libraries in the United States have formed consortiums. Member libraries pool the records

Figure 3.1 (continued)

Subject Card

```
Colleges and Universities--
United States--Entrance
Examinations

378.1056          Ranking, Morris
RAN

Getting into the top 100
colleges.
New York:  E-Z In School Press,
1993.  338 pp.
```

Subject Card

```
College and Universities--
United States--Directories

378.1056          Ranking, Morris
RAN

Getting into the top 100
colleges.
New York:  E-Z In School
Press,
1993.  338 pp.
```

This figure illustrates how one work, Getting into the Top 100 Colleges, is accessible by author, title, and two subject heading records. It can be located in the collection by the classification number, indicated on all four records.

of their catalogs into one database so that once one library has cataloged a book, all members can then follow that model.

The largest of these consortiums is the Online Computer Library Center (OCLC) in Dublin, Ohio. As of this writing it has over thirty million records for materials in libraries in the United States and other countries. It is among the most powerful retrieval systems in the world for locating American library items. Members of the consortium pay fees for its maintenance. Nonmembers may use the database on a pay-per-search basis. As you read this book a year or so after its release, OCLC will have grown by many millions of records, becoming even more effective.

Just as American librarians have established consortiums for cooperative cataloging, you as an adviser also understand the time and expense that library cataloging involves. Advisers who wish to follow library cataloging for their

Figure 3.2
Dewey Decimal Classification System

Table 1

100's	Philosophy
200's	Religion
300's	Social Sciences
400's	Languages
500's	Pure Science
600's	Applied Science
700's	Arts
800's	Literature
900's	History and Biography

Table 2

Literature

Second digit indicates national type		Third digit indicates genre	
800	General	1	poetry
810	American	2	drama
820	Anglo-Saxon	3	fiction
830	Germanic	4	essay
840	French	5	speeches
850	Italian	6	letters
860	Iberian	7	satire & humor
870	Latin	8	miscellaneous
880	Greek	9	other
890	Other		

Books of poetry end in 1 (before decimal point). French poetry is 841; Spanish poetry, 861; Greek poetry, 881. American fiction is 813; Greek fiction, 883. Numbers after the decimal point indicate historical periods and then specific writers within them. English drama is 822. Such drama during the period of Queen Elizabeth I is 822.3, and Shakespeare is 822.33.

collections can do so. Indeed, the larger a collection becomes, the greater are the needs of control and organization for retrieval.

However, for advisers with standard advising collections, the advantage of library cataloging comes from knowing its basic principles and techniques for organizing and retrieving materials. An adviser should take from these what is usable for advising. Let us, therefore, go from library cataloging to cataloging for advising.

CATALOGING FOR ADVISING

To determine what areas of library cataloging an advising center can use, we must consider what an adviser and advisee need in terms of retrieving information from an advising collection. We have seen that one of the principal ways in which libraries organize materials is by subject, because users generally search in libraries for material related to a particular topic. Such searching, of course, also happens in an advising center. An advisee comes to a center wanting to know about a particular kind of study: English courses in the United States, graduate study in architecture, or short courses in computer-aided design.

To facilitate access to resources for advisees on their study preferences, advisers should organize materials along the main categories of types or levels of study. For books, there can be a section of shelves for each of the main areas of study: English courses, short courses, elementary and secondary education, high school exchange, technical education, undergraduate study, graduate study, financial aid, predeparture orientation, return country readaptation, and whatever other areas are predominantly sought at your advising center. If you, for example, also respond to Americans wanting to study in your country, you need shelves for works regarding local undergraduate and graduate study, language courses, financial aid, and so on. College catalogs can be organized by those which are general and those specific to a certain discipline or profession.

The above treats subject organization of book material. Pamphlets, brochures, and other paper matter describing study for the above fields and categories can be organized in files and stored in filing cabinets, known in libraries as vertical files. File material will thus reflect the same subject divisions as the shelf material. Advisers and advisees will have easy access to shelf material. Initially, file material may not be as easy for advisees to orient themselves to and thus may require more reliance on advisers or staff in using it.

Nonprint materials are generally not as plentiful as print materials in an advising center. Audio and videotapes, microfiche, and compact discs can be kept with the equipment to use them.

Once an item is in its subject section, it can then be placed in alphabetical order. In library cataloging we have seen that this alphabetizing is based on the author's last name. However, in ordering books, we have also seen that advising materials often do not have individual authors and are more identified by their title—or sometimes by just some keyword in the title, such as "College Board" or "MBA." For advising purposes, therefore, it is more appropriate that materials be alphabetized by title rather than author.

Knowing some standard rules for alphabetizing is an important consideration. There are two methods of alphabetizing: letter-by-letter and word-by-word. In the first system alphabetizing occurs across a word and a phrase of words. It goes across the space between words. In the second, alphabetizing occurs only in relation to the first word of a phrase. It stops at the space between words.

Letter-by-Letter	Word-by-Word
raw	raw
rawhide	raw skin
raw skin	rawhide
red	red
reddened	red dye
red dye	reddened

Although letter-by-letter is an often-preferred method, word-by-word is used throughout libraries. It is important to be aware of both types, not only in order to have one's own method but to follow a different one of others. Several other things to note are:

1. Ignore initial articles. "A," "an," or "the" as a first word are ignored.
2. Symbols (+) and numerals (10, 101) should be considered as words, "plus," "ten," and filed accordingly.
3. Groups of letters, such as GRE, SAT, or TOEFL, should be interfiled as words.
4. Punctuation does not affect alphabetizing.

For a complete elaboration of the rules for alphabetizing, you may consult chapter 17 of *The Chicago Manual of Style*, 14th edition.

Location of Items in the Collection

Previously I mentioned that the cards used to make records of orders can be transferred to the record file of your collection, the collection catalog. Doing so means affixing a location code on the item. This code could be a Dewey Decimal number, which tells precisely what and where an item is. However, this is a difficult system to apply. Most advising centers can achieve the same objectives of classifying and locating an item, yet use a much easier and more basic code.

Since materials have been organized by subject and then arranged alphabetically, the location code, just as a DDC number, should reflect this pattern. Going back to Figure 2.6, the book ordered was a *Guide to Financial Aid for*

College. One section of books in an advising collection invariably is for financial aid. Therefore, a location code can indicate that section.

Rather than write out "financial aid" as the location section, a standard abbreviation, "fin aid," can be used. The location code appears not only on the catalog card but also on the item itself, usually at the base of the spine or, if that is not wide enough, in the lower left corner of the front cover. Subject location codes will vary among centers but normally include shelves for primary and secondary, technical, undergraduate and graduate education, English courses, financial aid, predeparture orientation, and so forth.

This subject designation is, however, only one part of the location guide. Since books are being organized on shelves in alphabetical order by title, the letter "G" should appear under the subject code so that the book can be more quickly found and regularly returned correctly to the shelf. Figure 3.3 shows the locator guide in the collection catalog once a work has been received and then been given its location code label.

Since by their appearance college catalogs identify themselves fairly obviously and an advising center can be dominated by such books, labeling them may not be necessary, and considerable time saved in not doing so. For ease of finding, though, general and special catalogs should be organized separately since it is by the level and type of study that these are sought by advisees. The general catalogs can be organized alphabetically by the name of the school, or they can be organized by state and then within state by name of school. Organizing by state can be helpful because this is a type of subject often of interest to an advisee (wanting, for example, to study in California or New York.).

The special catalogs can be organized by subject discipline: business, law, medicine, music, nursing, and so on. Within each discipline, organization can then occur alphabetically by name of school. Since some of these catalogs can be rather thin (almost like pamphlets), they may not be easily maintained on book shelves. In this case, they can be placed in file boxes or on a shelf or table. File boxes for this kind of material can be obtained from library supply vendors, mentioned earlier.

An important point should be made about maintaining things in order, an activity which consumes precious time. It is possible that for the specialized catalogs from architecture, music, nursing, or some other schools, one only has a dozen or so items. These do not have to be maintained in alphabetical order because it is as easy for a user to find something by flipping through them as by going alphabetically through them. The only purpose of order is to facilitate access. If there are situations in which access is facilitated without it, so much the better.

In considering the catalogs of specialized schools, there is another type of discipline-specific material that can be subject organized. At the graduate level we have seen that numerous professional organizations publish guides or directories to schools for study or research in their field. There are works such as *Graduate Medical Education Programs*, the *Guide to Architecture Schools*, and

Figure 3.3
Locator Guide on Catalog Card and Book

```
┌─────────────────────────────────────────────────────────────────┐
│ ┌──────────┐        Guide to Financial Aid for College, 45th     │
│ │ FIN AID  │        ed., 1994                                     │
│ │          │                                                      │
│ │ G        │                                                      │
│ └──────────┘                                                      │
│                                                                   │
│ Ordered:   22 Feb 94                                              │
│                                                                   │
│ Arr:   6 Jul 94                                                   │
│                                                                   │
│ Notes:   --Letter from publisher 23 Mar 94 saying book sold       │
│ out.  Will inform of new printing.                                │
│ --Note from publisher 20 May 94 saying second printing            │
│ being done.  Will send order.                                     │
└─────────────────────────────────────────────────────────────────┘
```

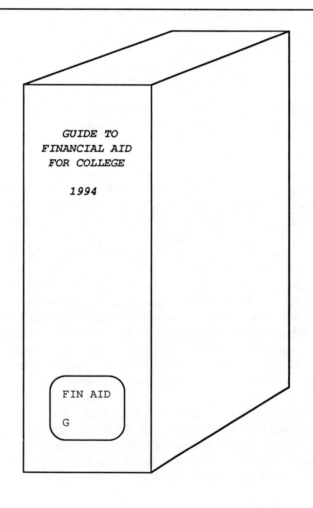

the *Official Guide to MBA Programs*. Rather than organize these in alphabetical order by title, it may be more convenient for their users to find them in order by their discipline. Thus the above works, rather than being organized on a shelf by the order of "D," "G," and "O," could appear under Medicine, Architecture, and Business. Their spine label would have "Grad" as the subject section code, and underneath it Medicine, Architecture, and Business as the subspecialization and shelf space locator. Indeed, depending upon how many of these directories or guides you have in your center, they might be kept in a subsection of graduate study on shelves just for these specialized works.

Incidentally, almost all of these guides have subject or specialization indexes. It can be helpful for advisees if you affix a small notice on the cover of the guide indicating the page on which such an index appears. This is one of the first things a user should be alerted to insofar as it is of primary interest to so many.

Pamphlets, brochures, and other materials comprising sheets of paper were previously mentioned as being organized in files and cabinets. There may be fields for courses in financing, marine sciences, marketing, and naval architecture; others, for graduate financial aid, health insurance, visas, and so on. Depending on the amount of time available in your office, you may want to keep this material in order alphabetically by institution or agency. To facilitate such order, underlining or using a markover pen to indicate the institution or agency helps in allowing one to identify the key element organizing the file. When received, this material should also be dated. Often there is no other way to identify when it was produced.

The multiple copies of brochures which come from English courses and to some extent from high school exchange programs can be organized and stored on shelves or in filing cabinets. However, rather than going through shelves or files to examine them, one can arrange samples of them in an album. Such an album can be another adviser-produced item. It consists of transparent envelopes or folders (like those in certain photo albums) placed in a binder. An album for English courses has one copy of the brochure for each course. The brochures can be arranged in the album first by state and then, within each state, by city. Locale is often a principal subject interest to advisees for English courses. Those courses which are specialized (for business, international trade, computers, secretaries, etc.) can be filed under such specializations. After examining sample brochures in an album, advisees can obtain their own copies from the multicopy supply stored in files or on shelves. If the sample is the only copy, a photocopy can be made.

Signage

Not only subject division and alphabetical ordering are important for facilitating access by users to an advising collection. Signage (visual communication by signs) is of paramount importance. Several practices in making signs are fundamental for successful visual communication and the orientation of a library user or advisee.

In signage it is crucial to remember that not just the letters of words on a background communicate something. If the size, the slant, or the type of letters change, if the color or type of background paper or plastic change, a viewer (persons looking at signs are as much viewers as readers) may think that these changes are also elements of the message. For example, if I write PART OF THIS SENTENCE IN UPPER CASE and then another part underlined, you will think some special attention is to be given to those parts. However, if as you read on you perceive there is no distinction to be given those parts, you are perplexed and question for what purpose the typographical alterations were made.

In an environment in which signs exist to give orientation to areas of the collection as parts of the advising center, their design must be as uniform as possible. Multiple signs for orientation require a uniform pattern of expression so that a user easily and continuously grasps the message of orientation. A slight deviation from the perceived pattern, something suddenly changing from block to cursive letters or underlined ones, or going from white to a gray background, signals to the viewer that something beyond an orientation message may be meant. The viewer wonders if there may now be something of urgency, special importance, or organizational sloppiness in the signs.

Signs for a section of catalogs, the different divisions of the book shelves, or a display of handouts should maintain a uniform signal of orientation. If black lettering is chosen for signage, that color should be maintained without. If capital letters and a certain style of forming letters are used, then that system should be maintained. If white paper is the background for signs, that color should be continued.

Changes in the system of visual communication should be a sign of some change in what is being communicated. For example, should variety in the examples of the previous paragraph be wanted, it should be in subsystems of communication, such as one system of color and style for catalogs, another for reference books, and another for file material. Perceiving a system is the key element in a viewer's being secure about what is being communicated. We discussed the possibility that books in the section for graduate study might be separated in terms of specialized guides and general graduate study directories. If the sign for the graduate section is in capital letters (also known as upper case), then the division of that section can be conveyed either by signs in smaller capital letters or using letters that have both upper and lower case.

Useful aspects of signage concern the vocabulary related to letter printing, displayed in Figure 3.4. Point refers to the size of letters, ten-point being a size commonly encountered in books, thirty-six or forty-eight in signs. Font refers to the design of letters. "Times" is a font one often finds in newspapers, "Courier" in typewriters. Style indicates how letters are written, in italics, underlined, or bold. Case refers to the use of capital and/or small letters, upper being capital

Figure 3.4
Aspects of Lettering for Signage

Point Size for Letters

A A A A A A A

9 10 12 14 24 36 48

Font:
Courier

Point size may vary by font.

Font Types

A   A   **A**   A

Courier   Times   Chicago   Monaco

Size: 24-point

Style of Lettering

ABC   *ABC*   <u>ABC</u>   ABC

Bold   Italics   Underlined   Shadow

Font: Courier, 18-point

Letter Case

UPPER CASE

          Upper and Lower Case

                    lower case

Font: Helvetica, 12-point

Point refers to the size of letters while font
indicates their design. Style is how letters are
written; case refers to use of capital and small
letters. (This comment is written in Courier,
10-point.)

letters; lower case, small letters. Block lettering refers to writing in all capital letters. For some examples of application of visual consistency in an advising environment, see Figure 3.5. *A Sign System for Libraries*, by Mary S. Mallery and Ralph E. Devore and published by ALA, is a useful book to consult on signage in libraries, containing many examples.

Electronic Database Organization

We suggested previously that certain advising functions, such as a contact file or orders for materials, could be made into a computer database—a computer program for organizing a body of information of a similar nature.

The catalog of the collection is a premier item to be converted into such an electronic resource. All the cards in your catalog can be keyed in as records in the database. Every day more libraries advance toward having computer catalogs, rather than the card variety. Although at one time this momentum was dominated by large libraries, even small libraries are today advancing with computerized catalogs.

In an electronic database one is relieved of the extensive and time-consuming requirements of organizing retrieval of information based on standardized access points. Depending on the program, an electronic database allows one to search either by certain fields of information in the database or by any word in it. One can search fields for publishers and authors and find all works by one author and the same company. One can search for all records having the word "grants" in them or "GRE" or "business." If you have three books in your collection with "GRE" in the title, these will appear along with their location information. Such searching by keyword in the title is, in effect, also a form of very specialized subject searching. However, the keyword must be in the title for the record and the work to be retrieved.

In the database of quite large collections, you can imagine that a certain problem may occur. If one searches for the keyword "business," thousands of records will be retrieved; and one can be as lost with so much data as before one's search. However, by refining the search, by making it express more specifically what one wants, this problem is reduced. One can add "international" to "business" or change "business" to "marketing."

In an advising center the volume of records for a database is normally such that a keyword is not so likely to pull up a mass of unwanted items ("false hits" in information science jargon). However, if you have, for example, entered all business school catalogs as records, each one with "business" in the title, each of these will come up. You must then add a delimiting keyword (such as Stanford or New York) to arrive more closely at what you want. However, in an average advising center that is well organized in terms of subject sections and shelf location and has effective signage reflecting this organization, it may be easier and quicker to go to the shelves to find an item than to search a catalog

Figure 3.5
Examples of Visual Consistency

GENERAL CATALOGS

Financial Aid

<u>Adviser's Office</u>

These signs have such variety, in bold, upper case, and underlined that the changes can send confusing messages to a viewer.

The same signs in uniform upper case use the consistency of lettering in order to underscore that they are all related to information about location within the advising center.

GENERAL CATALOGS

FINANCIAL AID

ADVISER'S OFFICE

If upper case seems too bold then upper and lower case can be used.

General Catalogs

Financial Aid

Adviser's Office

Italics can suggest a more elegant visual environment.

General Catalogs

Financial Aid

Adviser's Office

or database. In such an advising center, the latter tools are certainly more useful when searching for numerous items.

Which electronic databases should an advising center use? Considering the global scope of advising for international education, the database which first comes to mind is that developed by the United Nations Educational, Scientific, and Cultural Organization (UNESCO) and used by libraries around the world for control of acquisitions, cataloging, and circulation of books: the Integrated Set of Information Systems (ISIS). For small operations, there is MicroISIS. The great advantage of this system is its ease of usability, global availability through UNESCO, and low cost due to its development as a public service for library and information systems in developing and developed countries. A work which advisers might find useful is *Data Bases for Special Libraries: A Strategic Guide to Information Management* (Westport, Conn.: Greenwood Press, 1991) by Lynda W. Moulton.

We have examined the organization of advising materials in order to provide maximum facility for their retrieval by advisers and advisees. Looking first at library cataloging, in its rudiments, we saw the key principles of organization of materials by subject and then by specific identity of an item for location and retrieval. Out of the formalities of library cataloging we emphasized subject classification and location by alphabetical order as aspects relevant to cataloging for advising. Having thus seen how to organize for retrieval the extensive amount of materials acquired through collection development, let us now see how to fulfill our primary objective—communicating information to the advisee.

4

Communicating Information

In the previous chapter we concentrated on the organization of advising resources for their retrieval. We examined the concepts and procedures of cataloging, especially classification and filing, together with the maintenance and
relevance of these practices. We now come to reference service, which I consider
the fundamental activity of librarianship.

Why else have we tried to gather so many resources, organize them for retrieval, and manage their maintenance? All of these resources have been brought
together in order to be used by someone with specific information needs. Communicating what is in these resources and how to use them gives reference
service its fundamental value. The main object of our work as information professionals has been reached.

The importance of advising reference work cannot be underestimated; it may
even be described as vital. Decisions of advisees reached through dialog with
an adviser and research in advising resources will have a fundamental influence
on an advisee's life. Choosing a college is in some respects almost as critical a
decision as choosing a marriage partner, insofar as both have consequences for
one's personal, social, economic, and professional future.

At its heart reference service is an individualized and extensive operation of
communication. Reference work is the service by which librarians answer the
inquiries of library users or orient them to the sources which will have the
information they seek. In this chapter, therefore, we are going to examine how
as advisers we understand what a person wants. We then must see how to
respond to these wants and to communicate with advisees individually and in
groups. We shall examine how advisers accompany advisees in reaching their
information objectives. At the same time, we will examine how advisees can
become less dependent on advisees for acquiring information and more self-

sufficient in this regard. Finally, we want to see how the advising center can reach out in its community to communicate its important educational resources to those who need to know.

FINDING OUT WHAT AN ADVISEE WANTS TO KNOW

Listening to Clarify: The Short Reference Interview

Before considering the techniques whereby we communicate what information is available from advising resources, we must be aware of the techniques for understanding what a person wants from us. Consider for a moment the following exchanges between an individual and a reference librarian or an adviser.

Exchange Number One

User: Do you have a dictionary?

Respondent: Yes, there's one right over there on the top shelf of the reference section.

User: Thank you.

Exchange Number Two

User: Do you have a dictionary?

Respondent: Yes, let me show you the reference section. Can I help you find a word?

User: Oh, I'm not looking for a word. I thought it might have a table to show the difference between meters and yards.

Respondent: Let's see. This dictionary doesn't have that, but here's an almanac that does. Yes, here's a table of equivalency for distances.

User: Oh, thanks so much.

Exchange Number Three

User: Do you have a dictionary?

Respondent: Yes, we do in the reference section. Let me show you. Can I help you find something?

User: I need to see a table of equivalency for meters and yards.

Respondent: I'm not sure this dictionary has that. Let's check the almanac. O.K., here it is in the distance equivalency section. Will this be enough?

User: Yes, this will help. I'm writing a study plan for admission to graduate engineering school at a California university. I'm trying to explain what I did on a highway construction project as an intern for my civil engineering degree here.

Respondent: Oh, we have a book on the application process at American schools; and it includes models of study plans. We have a handout, too, which shows how to write study plans. Would you like to see these?

User: Yes, indeed. I never imagined there would be such material to ask for.

What has happened in these exchanges? At the end of each user's search objective (a dictionary, a table of distance equivalencies), the respondent who asked if anything further was needed ("Can I help you find a word?"; "Is this enough?") led the user to arrive further at what he or she needed. Actually, one can even imagine an extension of the third exchange.

Respondent: Do you need anything else for your application process?

User: Is there anything here that I could show one of my teachers about how to write a letter of reference for an American university?

Respondent: Yes, we have this handout. Anything further?

User: No, thanks so much. This is enough for now.

Of course, at the end of the second exchange, the user could have said, "Great, equivalencies are right here on the inside cover of this dictionary. Thanks a lot." A respondent might have added, "Is there anything else?" and the user said, "No, now I've got enough to understand some tables in an American textbook I'm reading."

The lesson of these exchanges is that the user or advisee was able to get to what was needed based on the skill of the respondent (the librarian or adviser) to keep the inquiry going until the user (the advisee) could say the search was over. It was not the librarian or adviser who assumed so.

Within librarianship, the above exchanges within reference service are known as reference interviews. The examples here are of the short variety. The skill of the reference interview is to allow the user to advance to his or her ultimate information need. Why must an information professional be so concerned with this? Consider the following:

User: Do you have an encyclopedia?

Respondent: Yes, here's one. Can I help you look something up?

User: I want to see the article on copper.

Respondent: Here we are. We have a section of books on copper. Would you like to see those too?

User: No, I'm trying to make bracelets; and I just want to see how to mold copper.

Respondent: Well, would you like to see some books on making copper crafts?

User: Yes, please.

Notice how an initial request for an encyclopedia was really a search for information on making copper bracelets. Why didn't the person ask for this to begin with? The answer lies in search strategy. People not only have information needs or objectives; they also have ways they have formulated by which they think they can satisfy their needs, reach their objectives.

Getting to the Right Strategy

The problem is that many people are not aware of all the innumerable ways to get to what they want. They may actually know only one. The crucial professional role of the librarian is to have a knowledge of those numerous ways and communicate them to those in need. The exhilaration of a library user in leaving a library with just what he or she sought is not just the satisfaction of an objective met, but the knowledge of a new means to reaching that and other objectives.

In asking to be of further assistance, librarians are not just helping to find information; they are also testing the adequacy of a user's search strategy to find information. What persons say they want is often just the means—the strategy—they have conceived for obtaining it. It can be an adequate or inadequate search strategy; the librarian has to test by maintaining communication.

Strategies by users can also be quite adequate. If a user wants to know about gold, and that an article in an encyclopedia will satisfy his or her inquiry, then objective and search strategy have matched. When the librarian asks, ''Anything else?'' the user can say, ''No, this is it.'' The librarian can close the interview knowing the user wants to end it.

One can never assume that what a person states as an objective—whether an encyclopedia, a dictionary, or an engineering study guide—is or is not an adequate search strategy. One asks to be of help in order to verify that persons have obtained what they sought. The librarian must be sure that a person is not searching for an objective which is really an inadequate means to some other end due to a limited knowledge of resources (that is, the means or strategies) for searching.

The relevance of the objectives and techniques of the reference interview for advising is multifold. It is almost unimaginable that a foreigner to American education, or any other national system, would know all the resources for obtaining study or research opportunities. At most some may know one or a few small pieces of the process—a scholarship, a TOEFL score—then fix on them as the objective, the exclusive means, of entering a U.S. university.

In interviewing, a great part of what one is almost always doing with the advisee is clarifying what the objectives are, explaining the means to them, and indicating resources for those means and to those objectives. The adviser is doing what a librarian does in a specialized reference interview.

Listening to Clarify: The Longer Reference Interview

What are some further techniques that an adviser can use to make sure that an advisee is fully communicating objectives? We have seen that variations on ''Can I help you further?'' or ''Is that enough?'' are one way; but many advising interviews are not about finding research resources. Financial background, academic history, knowledge of English, and family matters are frequently discussed. While statements offering help may play a part in these interviews, other questions and techniques must occur. An adviser will have to ask "why" many times. Why financial need; why better English; why is a test score inadequate; why Harvard or Berkeley? An adviser may thereby appear intrusive, inhibiting the advisee's communication. Variations of "why" can be used. "What would be the reason for this?" "What makes you consider that?" "For what purpose is that?" Moreover, one can encourage an advisee to elaborate upon a statement by repeating it to the individual as a question or as a concise restatement, encouraging a reply that elaborates upon the earlier information.

In the following exchange, notice how the adviser, who is well aware of the crucial importance of financing for study in the United States, uses techniques that obtain more information on this matter without seeming intrusive.

Advisee: I know how expensive college in the United States is; but my older brother has a job now with an import company in New York City; and I can cut my expenses by living with him.

Adviser: Living with your brother will be less expensive.

Advisee: Yes, he misses our family and has asked me to come and live with him and study there. He wants to help with my tuition, too.

Adviser: What a great opportunity. He will be paying your tuition?

Advisee: Yes, he says there are two types of tuition in public universities in the United States. If you live in the state, you pay much less.

Adviser: Yes, those are called in-state resident tuition rates. Each state has different regulations to determine who qualifies for them. Let's look at those for New York.

Here, through concisely restating and then making a question of the advisee's statements, the adviser has unobtrusively tested to see the extent of the viability of financial support in this case. Finding one point, however, the advisee's assumption of being an in-state resident, the adviser shows the advisee the qualifications for this status by examining the relevant college catalogs, and what replanning and estimating may have to be done.

Clarification can also occur using open-ended questions. These are questions stated in such a way as to require a full answer, not yes or no or a one-word reply. Examples of such questions include: "Could you give me examples?" "What do you mean?" "Can you explain that?" "How did you become interested in that?"

Other ways of encouraging the advisee's talk are through gestures and a relaxed attitude—nodding one's head, moving a hand, using affirmative words, such as "yes" or "of course," smiling, and joking.

There are also some exercises one can employ to heighten and check one's attentiveness to advisees. Those that involve three people can be quite helpful. The three rotate as adviser, advisee, and observer. In one exercise the adviser must relate, after an interview of five to ten minutes, all of the main points of the advisee's conversation. In another, the adviser remembers all of the physical movements and gestures of the advisee; in another, the adviser recounts all the references the advisee made regarding what he or she wanted to do and how to go about it. Such exercises not only heighten awareness to what and how things are being said but also expand the perspectives from which such exchange can be viewed. In these exercises each person successively plays each role. An adviser is him or herself then an advisee and then an observer of the advising interview.

Much about interviewing in advising seems to have come from personal counseling, even psychotherapy. I question some of the relevance of these disciplines for the advising dialog. Their objectives for interviewing do not correspond in many points with the objectives for advising. In counseling and psychotherapy, one interviews in order to obtain information about emotions and feelings which are often operating in a dysfunctional manner and/or environment. In advising, one is trying to find out about progressive awareness of objectives and resources for a functional goal of study or research in the United States or another country. Such ambition has its emotions and feelings; but they are part of the goal, not the subject of it. They are only of concern in advising as they interfere with that objective. If so, the advisee no longer has a reason for educational advising and should then possibly be referred to a counselor or psychotherapist. Interviewing in educational advising is of an objective, informational nature. Interviewing in personal counseling and psychotherapy is done to obtain subjective emotional data.

Counseling, of course, takes many forms. There is marriage counseling, job counseling, even gene counseling. One type of counseling and its interviewing experience are of singular relevance for advising, vocational counseling, or guidance. Indeed, much educational advising is sought in order to enhance career goals and professional activities. Vocational guidance expertise can be a key complement to adviser expertise as an information professional.

One often hears of listening skills as being important for interviewing. However, our attentiveness to a person must be combined with skills to stimulate communication so that there is a full record of information to which we can listen, to which we can be attentive. Listening skills are actually rather passive and inadequate unless accompanied by techniques which increase communication and the ability to have more to listen to and examine. We must come to think not so much of listening techniques but of "hearing more" skills.

Always, as one advances with further information in an advising interview, one can remember the lessons of the reference interview. A person may be stating an objective which is a limited or inadequate strategy for reaching an objective. This circumstance is especially true for educational advisees, foreigners to the culture and education of the United States or another country. They are trying to grapple with the enormous complexities of a different system and its varied resources. Thus, for example, the advisee who wants initially to know only about scholarships for a graduate diploma in urban sociology must also learn about other types of financial aid besides scholarships, as well as the nature of graduate degrees; and no doubt also has to become aware of interdisciplinary urban studies programs not within sociology departments that can offer what is being sought.

Laura Epstein's *Talking and Listening: A Guide to the Helping Interview* is a useful book for educational advising. Written by a social worker, it breaks interviewing down to the basic components whereby it is usable in a variety of professional applications. For libraries and information centers, see also *The Reference Interview as a Creative Art* by Elaine and Edward Jennerich, which includes many exercises and examples.

Ambience for Dialog

More than what an adviser says to enhance an interview will determine its success. Factors of environment—of ambience—are also important. To an advisee exploring the landscape of the advising center, you, the adviser, are the most important "piece" on the horizon. The advisee concentrates on you as the potential vehicle to satisfying many goals and ambitions. In professional encounters, therefore, we want to be as attentive to the inquirer as he or she is to us.

But our attention is not so much focused on the person as what we do for the person: listening and encouraging conversation, noting what is said, showing how to use a book or piece of equipment, and checking up on research. Thus dialog, or exchange, is achieved between adviser and advisee: talking with each other, then working together. This interaction forms the axis—the norm—of the advising environment.

Nonetheless, there are advisees whom one focuses on as exceptional persons. They are the adrenalin of advising. There are young people, curious and resolute in wanting to find out about and study in another country; there are professionals with solid, original reputations who will benefit themselves and others through a cutting-edge opportunity in the United States; there are fascinatingly creative people—a print artist or a drama critic—for whom the experience abroad becomes one more facet of their allure. You, the adviser, are a unique witness to the experiences of these people, from the inception of the idea of foreign study, through application and acceptance, and on to departure, the experience abroad, and then return.

There are also inquiries which are not so compelling, which do not have the qualifications. Nevertheless, we maintain the axis of dialog and work with all until it is obvious that study or research abroad cannot occur. In these situations it is important to point out to such advisees that qualifications can be improved. English can become better; grades can be raised. A disappointment can then become an incentive for long-term enhancement of both study and career opportunities.

To sustain the advising environment with its axis of dialog and work together, one must be able to identify the satisfaction and enjoyment advising offers. This is as fundamental in sustaining the vigor of an adviser and the environment of an advising center as it is personal and varied. It is your sustaining reward from advising.

Since these are as personal as they are varied, I can only recount what I found to be rewards, and emphasize the importance of making such an assessment yourself. As I previously mentioned, there were the personalities of so many people about to be enhanced or reformed by the American study opportunity. To this, I found intriguing the variety of fields of study and professions one dealt with in advising. It was fascinating to see how foreign doctors or psychologists received their professional formation, and how that compared to and could be accommodated into the American pattern. It was fascinating to talk to a pianist wanting to know more about music recording courses, a Boy Scout interested in an English course for a worldwide jamboree, or a physicist concerned about nuclear armaments. It pleased me that people would open a part of their lives to me on considerations that were so personally important. I found it an enlivening privilege to observe this kaleidoscope of lives pursuing so many varied paths. I wanted to know what they wanted to know.

For me another great satisfaction was getting people together with just the source of information they needed. This situation could be as satisfying as it was at times surprising. I remember the delight (and amazement) of someone finding a course in shrimp harvesting; of another finding fashion design that was couturier and not prêt-à-porter; of others who were fascinated by the specializations offered in guides to chemistry, physics, psychology, sociology.

One's satisfaction and enjoyment in doing advising are the fundamental support for the axis of dialog and work with advisees, the heart of the advising environment. Other things, of course, comprise the advising environment. The previous two chapters were dedicated to fundamental parts of this environment: ample and up-to-date materials organized for efficient access by users. In addition, certain social and physical considerations must be recognized as part of the environment. For example, people should be greeted as soon as they enter an advising center. It says they are welcome and will receive attention.

If you advise sitting at a desk, let the advisee sit next to it. The desk should not be a barrier between you and the advisee, but a common surface which you share as you begin talking to each other and working together; showing, for example, how to use a book or fill out a test registration bulletin.

Mention should be made of decoration (a section in chapter 5 deals with organization of office space). Essentially, for encouraging a natural environment with economy and effectiveness, one cannot underestimate the value of windows and plants. Clear, changing light together with vegetation underscore everything about an environment being natural, harmonious, and at ease in human interchange. Concerning room lights, I personally do not like the harshness of overhead light; I prefer table lamps with their more evenly distributed light at a human level and on faces.

RESPONDING TO ADVISEES

Having examined the means by which we obtain information from advisees regarding their needs, let us now examine how we meet those needs. Earlier I pointed out ways to obtain complete information from advisees. At the time I think I may have heard a reader say, "You know, I don't really need to hear more from the people who come to me. It is already difficult enough to cope with the number of requests I now get. Dealing with that amount is what I really need to know about." Maybe that voice was just an echo of my experience when I first began to do advising, feeling overwhelmed by the requests (even pleas) for information.

Dealing with requests efficiently and thoroughly, and allowing more time to listen, is what we now want to examine. There is a sequence of steps one can follow in the course of advising to ensure that you have obtained full information from advisees, and that they have obtained full orientation from you. The first step is intake, acquiring initial, basic information from an advisee. This is followed by initial orientation for the type and/or level of study or research the person seeks. This stage involves advisees receiving general orientation handouts and possibly listening to an audio or videotape. It is followed by an interview with an adviser for individual treatment of the case. The outcome of this meeting will determine the final and usually longest stage: research by the advisee, adviser accompaniment of this research, and further interviewing.

Intake

The record of what an advisee needs and how a request has been responded to is not information advisers can carry around in their heads for all the advisees who consult with them. It is necessary to have a record of this information, a case history of the advising process with an individual from the first inquiry through the final one.

Figure 4.1 is a suggested model for keeping a record of advisee consultations. This form satisfies a vast array of inquiries. It can be completed as thoroughly by someone seeking a high school exchange program as by an individual seeking postdoctoral work. The advisee may have no knowledge of American education processes, or may know all about TOEFL or GMAT scores. The form is applicable as well to high school students seeking college study or professionals looking for short-term, continuing education opportunities. It also acknowledges and respects the fact that there may be some information an individual does not wish to give.

The front side of this form is for initial intake of information. The reverse side is used by the adviser or a staff member to record the nature of each advisee visit to the center. Thus the progress of the advising process is recorded, noting the content of interviews or the nature of research visits.

The form is shown here in English. However, as part of the initial orientation

Figure 4.1
Advisee Consultation Record

```
                  Educational Advising Center
Please fill out the following.  You need not complete items
not relevant to you or that you prefer not to answer.
                                              Today's
Name_____ Date_____
      Surname                  First Name
Address_____
Phone(s)                     Date of
Home_____ Off._____ Birth_____   ┌──────────────────┐
School or                                       │ Tests Taken      │
University_____ Major_____      │ Dates & Scores   │
Date of                                         │ TOEFL            │
Graduation_____ Profession_____       │ _____  _____   │
Current                                         │ SAT              │
Employment_____        │ _____  _____   │
Field of Study                                  │ GRE/Gen          │
Interest in U.S._____       │ _____  _____   │
Self-rating of Know-                            │ GRE/Spe          │
ledge of English_____        │ _____  _____   │
Source for Financing  Personal    Financial     │ GMAT             │
of Study (Check)      Funds_____ Aid_____      │ _____  _____   │
                                                │ Other(s)         │
                                                │ ____ ____ ____   │
                                                │ ____ ____ ____   │
                                                └──────────────────┘
```

--13 Jun 94 Received initial orientation regarding graduate
study. Advisee asked about financial aid. I explained that a
grad. study program in physics can be directly for doctorate,
which affects type of aid requested. Pointed out possible
sources on financial aid handout. Specialization is plasma
physics and she is in top ten percent g.p.a. of class. In third
year of study. Is about to complete certificate program of BNC
English course. Showed her use of Peterson's guide and one for
physics programs.
--15 Jun 94 Began research in guide to physics programs.
Listened to audio tape on use of college catalogs.
--20 Jun 94 Continued research. Discussed ten schools she is
interested in. We examined reasons.
--29 Jul 94 Narrowing selection to three: Berkeley, Texas, and
Michigan or Columbia.
--7 Sep 94 Picked up TOEFL and GRE registration booklets. Has
begun financial aid requests with two federal government
agencies. Discussed writing of study plan and gave handout with
model. Informed her that there are GRE and TOEFL preparation
guides--she has bought her own though.

process, an adviser may think it should be in the language of the local country, guaranteeing that an advisee understands the information being requested. Others might argue that the form should be in English in order to test whether the advisee is going to be able to deal with the multitude of English-language materials that will be part of the research and application process for study in the United States.

I prefer that the form be in the native language. Enough other opportunities will arise in the advising process for both the advisee and the adviser to evaluate the ability of using advising materials in English. The most important consideration at the time this form is completed is to make sure the individual knows what information to provide. Here the form is in English because that is the only language held in common among all the readers of this book.

Such advisee records are a prime candidate for organization in a computer database. As a card form they basically can only be retrieved by the surname under which they are alphabetically filed—or any other system used locally. As a database, information can be retrieved through various access points, such as field of study, date of graduation, or profession. Such retrieval allows automatic assembly of lists of advisees to be notified about potentially interesting occurrences, such as special orientation programs or the arrival of new publications of interest. The forms themselves can be somewhat used for this purpose, but that involves time-consuming coding with symbols or clips.

Initial Orientation

Once the advisee has completed the consultation record form, the adviser can direct him or her along the appropriate track of orientation. After checking the field of study which interests the advisee, the adviser knows how to track the initial orientation. This tracking routes advisees to standard modules of general or initial orientation information, guaranteeing that the advisee receives all the basic information needed to advance in the advising process while not taking the time of an adviser to repeatedly give out this information to each one.

The tracks for advisees comprise all the areas in which one gives advising. These will vary but usually include English study courses, high school exchange programs, technical and short-term study courses, and undergraduate and graduate study. For each of these areas one can prepare a standard module or packet of orientation. Part of this module will be a handout to be read by the advisee before consulting an adviser. The handout(s) can be accompanied by an audio or videotape.

The handouts and audiovisual aids contain systematic answers to all the standard questions advisees have at the beginning of the advising process. For university degree programs, these materials indicate the qualifications for a program or course, academically, financially, and personally. They also indicate what resources exist for finding a course and how to use them. They outline the costs and the types of financial aid available. The materials also detail the application process in terms of documentation and schedules.

These modules guarantee that advisees receive all the basic information necessary for the educational objective they are pursuing. Unlike advisers, these modules do not forget or skip certain parts. Once advisees have progressed through this stage, they come to an adviser needing only clarification of points not understood. At the same time, advisers have not had their time repeatedly occupied in personally giving this information.

This method of standardizing initial, basic information is known as point-of-access orientation. When persons have standardized initial questions about how a system or agency functions, an information depot is set up to act as a point of access for orientation, providing handouts together with an audio, video, or slide demonstration. In a library or museum, at points where inquiries cluster, handouts and an audio or videotape are available to give explanations and information.

Some advisers may not have audiovisual resources for point-of-access orientation, and must therefore give presentations themselves. In order to facilitate the adviser's time, group general orientation in each of the areas of advising can be scheduled, possibly on a weekly basis. Thus all areas from English courses to graduate study have a general orientation program at least once a week. An advisee receives the information handout before the session in order to read it and be prepared to absorb the program's information. The scheduling pattern for the sessions can be staggered from week to week in order to accommodate advisees' various commitments. Thus undergraduate orientation might be in the afternoon of the first Monday of the month, then in the next week on the morning of the second Tuesday, then the afternoon of the third Wednesday, and so on throughout the month for the various areas of group orientation.

Regardless of the methods used for orientation sessions, audiovisual presentations or adviser group orientation (or a combination of both), the script will follow the components previously mentioned: (1) the requirements for admission to courses, (2) reference resources for finding out courses, (3) costs, and (4) the application process.

A very important aspect to begin emphasizing for advisees at this stage is not just reference resources available, but how to use them. Of course, such instruction will be more extensive and specific during the first interview, as the viability of the study objective is explored. However, it is vital for the advisee to perceive from the very beginning the importance of doing one's own research into advising materials in order to find what courses to select. Choice will be made by the advisee, not the adviser. Information for this choice will be sought by the advisee from resources maintained by the center.

Orienting a library public regarding the use of research materials is referred to as user education. It is considered one of the fundamental parts of reference service. Not only must users be directed to the resources they require, they must also be shown, as necessary, how to use them. Such teaching can occur individually or in group sessions. In college libraries, user education classes are quite numerous at the beginning of each semester. They focus on various things: how to use the library's computer catalogs, what resources exist in special collections and how to use them (much like advising materials are a special collection), or how to use the library as a whole.

It is fundamental that advisers educate advisees in the use of materials. This importance arises not just from the fact that it is the advisee who chooses a course based on the body of information acquired in the research process. Also important is becoming self-reliant in the search for information. Such self-reliance is the beginning of adapting to the norms of education in the United States.

Educational advising occurs in countless cultures around the globe. Although an important part of American culture is self-reliance, this may not be such a concern in many other cultures which are more focused on social integration and interdependence, including the deference of the young to the orientation of the older. In these circumstances, user education (instruction for independent use of materials) may not be particularly recognized or even valued.

Nonetheless, an adviser for study in the United States must be very aware of how those studying in this country are expected to operate on their own. American culture is undoubtedly a helping one—just witness the enormous amount of volunteerism—but a great deal of the help it gives is information on self-help (that is, user education). A favorite citation of Benjamin Franklin, one of the authors of the American Declaration of Independence, was "God helps those who help themselves." An overseas adviser is doing advisees a serious disservice by not orienting those who will be going to study or research in the United States with adequate experience in pursuing information independently. Education is actually considered the main vehicle in American culture for achieving independence and self-reliance.

One must incorporate user education into advising from the earliest stages. This gives the advisee confidence in dealing with the complex process of finding, applying, and being admitted to an American school. It also prepares the advisee to operate within the cultural norms of the educational system being sought.

Another cultural adaptation for an advisee may be initial orientation with audiovisual or group methods. In some cultures people show that they are attentive to a request by always communicating person-to-person. An adviser, in using less direct, though thorough, mechanical methods for giving initial orientation, is already showing an advisee not just information about American education but a norm of the educational culture in which one must function.

Having seen the rationale, modes, and components of initial orientation, let us now look at the first individual interview between adviser and advisee.

First Individual Interview

The purpose of the first interview with an advisee changes in the course of its conduct. Initially one needs to know the viability of the advisee's objective for study in the United States. Once that is considered, one can advance to beginning orientation for research for that study objective.

For someone seeking higher education in the United States, there is essentially a series of basic questions determining the viability stage of the interview. They are concerned with knowledge of English and with financial and academic qualifications. The answers to these become the initial information noted on the advisee consultation record.

After greeting the advisee, one may begin by confirming from the now-completed advisee consultation record what the advisee considers his or her knowledge of English. It bears mentioning here that the interview should not be conducted in English because this may impede the flow of information, especially when a person may not only be ill at ease in that language but also in being interviewed. Staying in one's own language greatly facilitates the environment for being at ease in giving information.

Simple objective data can verify a person's English language qualifications. Since a TOEFL score of 500 or more is required for undergraduate or graduate study, a person will have to have studied English for several years in a sound program. The adviser should know which programs these are locally, and how to make an equivalency between their instruction and English language requirements. It is important to know if the advisee has any certificates or diplomas for English proficiency.

The initial orientation program will have told the advisee about the need for proficiency in English. For advisees seeking higher education, the program will have mentioned TOEFL and the scores needed on it. In the interview, therefore, the adviser does not have to explain TOEFL but can concentrate on giving the advisee an idea of how his or her knowledge of English will or will not meet that requirement.

If knowledge of English is far below adequacy and one sees from the consultation record that the person needs financial aid, which itself requires proficiency in English, the interview must now show the advisee what to do in order to become better prepared for study abroad. It is important to check if financial aid is needed. Finance questions can be the next stage of the interview. Indeed, if not appearing too abrupt, they can be the opening questions. Occasionally individuals indicate a need for financial aid, but on finding that such a request may impede a study opportunity they reconsider their resources, such as relatives, and change to wanting to finance their study from personal resources.

In dealing with finances, if the person is requesting financial aid, he or she must know that a high grade point average and admission test scores will be required. One must also clarify that financial aid from an American school is not likely for a foreign student, especially at the undergraduate level. Local agencies for financial aid are more likely sources. As part of the packet of information for the initial orientation, the advisee should receive a handout indicating what local sources (both public and private) and types of financial aid are available. This handout generally becomes an adviser's most sought-after publication.

With advisees showing appropriate initial qualifications, one progresses to the second half of the interview: orientation in regard to how to find courses, to do research. In great part this becomes a user education tutorial.

In examining a book with an advisee, one should always show the title and give a brief description of its contents and purpose. If one is advising a person for graduate study in physics, then one should show the appropriate volume, for example, from Peterson's for the sciences and its section on physics. Together with the advisee, you should examine the table of contents to find the page for the appropriate section and specialization, letting the advisee use the work to find the right page, thereby getting a sense of beginning to use materials. You can point out one of several entries and show the type of information included such as address, communication numbers, and admission requirements.

If you have a computer program or compact disc which allows electronic searching of schools and programs, that will probably have been mentioned in the general orientation session. During the interview, one can give specifics about such searching and use of the equipment. If the machine itself cannot be used for demonstration because it is already in use, a model may be demonstrated or a point-of-access orientation tool created.

You may also have in your collection the *Graduate Programs in Physics, Astronomy, and Related Fields*, published by the American Institute of Physics. You will want to point out certain features of this work, such as the specialization index. You may look up together one or two institutions which you found in a previous guide in order to show the difference between that and this guide.

The advisee should also know that examination of graduate school catalogs will give more information on courses. You will want to indicate where these catalogs are in your collection and how they are available for use (paper copies, microfiche, and/or compact disc). A later stage of advising may sometimes be more appropriate to explain the use of catalogs in order to avoid information overload. For this reason an audiocassette and handout explaining the use of college catalogs can be a good point-of-access tool, allowing advisees to be informed of their use whenever they begin the phase of researching.

If you have books or articles which evaluate or rank graduate programs, you will want to inform the advisee of these, going through one of the works, allowing the advisee to find the section of preferred interest. Comment should be made about ranking information, in contrast to evaluation or assessment information, as potentially being misleadingly conclusive.

Throughout this tutorial, as one uses materials, their location in the center should be indicated. At the same time you will want to indicate your policy for coming to the center and doing research with open access to materials.

In order to aid advisees in beginning to organize and carry through the research for finding a program in the United States, you should give them a copy
of an application data record or worksheet, shown in Figure 4.2. This form
allows an advisee to uniformly note and organize application information for
each school examined and to which admission is sought. One can point out the
principal features of this form as a way of reviewing some of the main points
of the general orientation and the interview. The form reinforces what has been
said about admission deadlines and exams, costs of study, and supporting documentation such as letters of reference or exam scores. At least one copy of this
form or similar worksheet should be given to the advisee during the interview,
indicating where more are available in the center. One will be needed for each
of the schools the advisee examines as the research phase of advising begins.
These forms further serve as records, permitting the adviser to study the progress
of an advisee's research.

With initial orientation and the first interview over, an advisee may begin
research the same day or return to the center another time. The first interview
is the beginning of personal and individualized interaction between adviser and
advisee. It has been mentioned that the advisee form for recording application
data helps the advisee organize research and review the main points of the
application process. It also reinforces that it is the advisee's responsibility to
seek information and evaluate it for a decision about choosing a school.

Accompanying Research

With the first interview and all succeeding research, the axis of dialog and
work, the fundamental environment of advising, is achieved. It has really been
for this that all the other activities of collection development, organizing of
materials, and orientation have been conducted.

Each time advisees come to the center, they should be asked what they wish
to do and a decision made as to whether this requires further personal interviewing or orientation. The advisee consultation record will indicate these further visits and interviews. Certainly, if by the third visit an advisee has not again
spoken with the adviser, the adviser should ask how research is going and if
the advisee would like any of the application data records checked. The adviser
should also ask whether there have been any problems in using materials or
understanding processes, and check what other materials an advisee might need
to know about. At this stage, not only the application process has to be checked
but also any financial aid applications.

Ideally, advisees should be able to meet with an adviser as they choose.
Certainly in libraries one generally consults with librarians at will. However, all
advisers are familiar with the situation in which many people may be waiting
to see them as they are interviewing an advisee. Moreover, unlike in libraries,
even the first interview in advising is longer than a normal consultation with a
librarian. Actually, as one moves beyond basic user education orientation in

Figure 4.2
Advisee Data Record for Application to a College or University

> Somewhere City Educational Advising Center
> Data Record for Application to College or University

1. Name and Address of Institution

Phone   Fax   E-mail

Any Contact Person(s) with Address(es) and Communication
Number(s)

---

2. Admission Deadline   Fee   Exam(s) and
for Application   Score(s) Required

---

3. Tuition   Special Fee(s)   Room and Board

---

4. Type(s) of   Deadline(s) for   Additional Documen-
Financial Aid   Application   tation Required

---

5. Observations on Institution from
Adviser

Faculty or Alumni

Published Source(s)

---

6. Key Dates
      Taken
Exam(s)   Scores
      Results Received

                                        Given to Writers
Application   Letters of
Sent   Reference   Sent by Writers

---

7. Miscellaneous

Date above Research Begun   Principal Sources Used

libraries, it becomes necessary to schedule meetings with specialized librarians or bibliographers regarding individual research needs and the specialized library resources available to meet those needs.

In an advising center, even though one might wish to allow advisees to always have ready access to an adviser, a moment eventually occurs when the adviser has to divide time between open access and scheduled blocks of time. This decision will probably be made when one perceives numerous incidents in which open access, with many waiting advisees, is hindering their access to you. There are, of course, some advisers who may not deal well with continuous access by advisees and who want all meetings scheduled. The ultimate result of this practice may sometimes be to delay access and miss the timely need an advisee has for orientation.

An advisee should always be free to come to the center and use the collection. During an adviser's open access time, advisees can combine their research with consultation according to their turn. It is only during the adviser's scheduled interview time that there will not be this easier access.

How might scheduled and open access time be divided? Out of an eight-hour work day, an adviser will spend at least two to three hours in administration (that is, those things necessary to maintain the advising center). The more advisers a center has, along with secretarial and clerical staff, the less administration may fall to all advisers except for the head adviser. Outside of administration, the average adviser will probably have five to six hours per day for advising. Depending on the pressure for individual interviews and how much adviser time is used in general orientation (and here the value of videotapes becomes dramatically evident), one may be able to keep individual interviewing to two or a bit more hours per day. If interviews are scheduled for twenty-minute periods, an adviser will have time for about six or more interviews per day and the rest available for open access, with the exception of general orientation. An adviser's open access time should be posted in the center so that advisees who want open consultation time can organize their visits accordingly. It is assumed that scheduling will be staggered throughout the week in order to accommodate varying advisee schedules.

With so much concentration on interviewing, and recognizing the personal nature of much of the information conveyed in an interview, privacy in advising is paramount.

Given this fundamental activity in advising, interviewing requires that every adviser have his or her own office. If space limitations in an advising center prohibit this or, if in a one-person operation, the center itself is considered the adviser's office, there should be one corner screened off where such privacy can occur. Advisees must often talk about their personal financial circumstances, family situations, and academic performance. Without privacy they can feel inhibited from conveying information which may be crucial to the advising process. Arrangement of space for privacy will be discussed in Chapter 5.

A word of caution on reference service and the reference interview: research about reference service work has consistently found that a library user can be misled regarding the quality of the information received, depending on the manner in which he or she is treated by the librarian. In studies in which a user is warmly treated by one librarian and politely but unemotionally by another, the user will invariably judge the warmer treatment as the better service. This judgment is made even when the "warmer" librarian gives an incorrect or incomplete response and the unemotional librarian thoroughly and correctly answers the user. Warm is defined as being pleasant and smiling with users, agreeing over something, and possibly lightly touching them. In these cases a style that seems to help may actually fail to do so. Of course, a standard way by which we all check the sincerity of warmth is to note, after all the smiles and pleasant talk, how many excuses for something not being available or done begin to appear.

Being aware of this potential contradiction, advisers must guard against it for the foundation of their integrity as information professionals. One hopes that advisers can always be both warm and informative, showing that how they are is also what they are in terms of their professional service. The integrity of warmth must always be verified in the conveying of rigorously thorough and correct information to an advisee.

Advising Orientation Programs

So far we have examined advising as it very intensively pertains to the adviser. However, there are orientation programs one can organize with former advisees and alumni which are excellent advising vehicles. These programs bring together a panel of former advisees and alumni for an audience of those who are in the advising process or are considering the possibility of study abroad. The role of the adviser is one of organizer and possibly moderator of the program panel. The composition of the panel is determined by the theme of the program. One can have programs which are related to the experience of applying to a school. These may be at the undergraduate or graduate level or for specific areas of graduate study, such as business or engineering.

From my own experience in conducting such programs, a two-hour session should have at the most only four panelists. This allows time at the end of presentations for questions and discussion. Generally, during the program panelists should outline (1) how they researched to find schools and then applied to them; (2) how they obtained financial aid if they sought it; (3) what studying in the American academic environment was like; and (4) of what value the experience has been, personally and professionally, now that they have returned. Each panelist can go through this script individually; or, for more variety, the moderator can ask each part of the script as separate questions to the panelists.

Besides these specialized study orientation programs, others can be organized for predeparture orientation or for readaptation after return to the home country. The former program gives orientation to those who are about to depart for

American schools. A panel of alumni in this program relates the steps they followed to prepare for departure and adaptation to life in the United States. Readaptation programs are for those returning to their country and needing to acclimate themselves once again to its life and culture. Advisees should also be informed of predeparture or readaptation materials available in the advising collection.

One can also organize programs with panelists who studied English in the United States, went to high school there, or were in short-term study courses. A program with panelists describing just their experience with financial aid can prove a great crowd gatherer.

If you can videotape any of these programs, the tapes will be of use in orienting those who could not attend. Conducting these programs assumes an adviser has access to an auditorium. Publicity can be obtained through announcements at your center and through the communication network of messengers (to be described in the last part of this chapter).

The advising programs are a bit of work to produce although they become easier the more they are done. They are quite enjoyable for the youthful, concentrated audience they bring together. Immensely effective, they are quite gripping for the advisees because they relate experiences that are so immediate.

Advising by Mail

An adviser's mail will always have a certain number of advising inquiries. The more complex the need for advising, the inherently more inadequate such advising becomes, because the advisee is without access to the principal resources—an adviser and advising materials.

In this respect, therefore, the priority in responding to these inquiries is to see if the individual can visit an advising center. From the address, one may discern that the individual is in or near a city with a center, and one should inform the inquirer of that. The inquirer may actually be near your center. Near in this case can be defined as being no more than four hours away round-trip by car, bus, or train. Such inquirers should be encouraged to visit the advising center unless otherwise unable to do so.

For those inquirers who cannot reach you or another center, one can respond by sending the handouts used in general orientation. This material, followed by a phone call from the advisee, might allow the adviser to select and photocopy some material from guides and directories. Figure 4.3 gives examples of correspondence one can photocopy or store as files in a word processor as standard responses in advising by mail.

When advising by mail and phone is inadequate for a complex advising case (and possibly too expensive and time-consuming with postage, phone calls, photocopies, and faxes), the adviser has the duty to inform the person that only a personal visit to an advising center is appropriate. The earlier this is determined

Figure 4.3
Responses for Advising by Mail

```
        Cityville  Educational  Advising  Center
                 123  Education  Road
                 98765  Cityville
                    Country  X
        Phone  Number    Fax  Number    E-mail  Address
```

Date

Greetings:

Thank you for your recent inquiry regarding your
educational interest in the United States.
Insert No. 1:
Your inquiry can receive attention at an advising center in
your vicinity.   The address and phone number are:
The adviser is:
Insert No. 2:
Since you live within travel distance of this advising
center, we suggest that you visit us personally in order to
better serve your needs. If you decide to visit us, please
inform us beforehand so that we can make scheduling
arrangements for your inquiry. You may contact us via the
communication numbers indicated above. If a personal visit
is not possible, let us know and we will make other
arrangements to give you information.
Insert No. 3:
Enclosed please find the information you requested. Should
you need further assistance, feel free to contact us again.
The goal of studying in the United States is generally one
which requires intense research in educational advising
materials and consultation with an adviser. May we suggest
that if you have any opportunity to visit our center, it
would be greatly to your advantage in reaching your
educational goal.

Sincerely,

O. N. DeJobb,
Educational Adviser
_____

The above contains insertable texts for three different
letters.   The priority in these responses has been to
direct the advisee to an advising center. Insert three
sends information to someone not near any center but
emphasizes the importance of a consultation.

the better so that one does not become involved in a situation of increasingly complex advising which one cannot continue.

For further treatment of advising by mail, there is an excellent section on this topic in the College Board manual for overseas advisers, "Advising by Mail and Telephone," by Brigitte Birke-Dexheimer.

Electronic Communication

Increasingly, mail means electronic mail or e-mail. It offers more rapid and fluid communication than surface (or "snail") mail for dialog between adviser and advisee, a fundamental part of the advising process. It is still restricted as an advising vehicle because of limited access to advising materials. One can download and send an advisee word processor files of general orientation. We previously noted that some college catalogs are available on the Internet. Advisees can be informed of your contacts who have e-mail.

However, published guides to chemistry, dance, or English proficiency courses, short-term study, or financial aid are copyrighted material not yet freely accessible over a global network. Nonetheless, certain general reference works, dictionaries and almanacs, and literary classics are accessible. Electronic advising is developing; it is already better than surface mail, but is not yet an alternative to the advising center. As ways are found to put the most essential works of advising on a network, this action is going to give educational advising a strong new electronic dimension.

The term "virtual library" refers to the electronic system whereby a user finds a work at some library through a computer network of library catalogs, requests it electronically, receives and returns the item through interlibrary loan, possibly consulting along the line with a reference librarian by e-mail. Through an electronic network, numerous physical libraries become one collection, catalog, circulation system, and reference service—the virtual library. The "virtual educational advising center" is now in the making. It will have the axis of the advising environment, dialog with an adviser and research work in advising materials. However, everything will be conducted electronically. A decade from now, the revision of this guide may be a book, but it will certainly also be an electronic text giving instruction about many other electronic texts.

The Internet, the mammoth network of computer networks, proves daily to be one of the richest and most economical resources in electronic communication. Initially its value was primarily for e-mail. To find e-mail addresses of individuals at numerous organizations and places around the world, one accesses "whois" directories. However, as networks of specialized information (of which OSEASNet is one) increasingly grow on the Internet, its value has come to be in accessing these networks or electronic storage points of specialized information. (Note: one may often hear of Internet and Bitnet. The former is the larger system, developed by the U.S. government, especially the Department of Defense and the NSF, and used by government, academic, and various organizations throughout the world. Bitnet is primarily a communication network among university and research entities, beginning in the United States.)

Access to the Internet occurs through the computer service department of one's host organization or through private companies. One thereby not only has e-mail but the capacity to access active communication networks and electronic storage depots of information, known as "gophers."

Overseas advisers have such a gopher, storing directory data on advisers around the world along with articles and publications on advising. It is part of a larger database for NAFSA and international education subjects. One can telnet to it via gopher.colostate.edu or gopher.csc.fi. You can always identify an Internet address by the code in which it ends. For the United States, addresses always end in three-letter codes such as "gov," "edu," or "org," indicating government, academic, or some other organizational affiliation. Outside the United States, addresses end in a two-letter code indicating the country location. Thus Canada is "ca," France is "fr," and Germany is "de" (for *Deutschland*). The address above ending in "fi" is for Finland.

Networks, gophers, and directories multiply daily on the Internet. To partially index them, an archiving service called "archie" exists. Not only text but also sound and pictures are available on the Internet through the world-wide web (WWW) and the Mosaic interface.

This variety of resources and the means to access them show the singular potential of the Internet and electronic communication for the immediate and long-term prospects of advising and all information services. By finding a network of plastic surgeons one can put an advisee wanting to specialize in such surgery into contact with a network of expertise on the subject. Previously we saw how NSF publications can be acquired electronically. The Colorado Alliance of Research Libraries (CARL) maintains a current contents index of scholarly journals in all disciplines called CARL UnCover. One can search it by keyword to find the principal specialists publishing in a particular field. Thereby an advisee can know by whom and where certain specialized study and research is being done. It is accessible at various sites found via archie. The Library of Congress has a gopher (accessed via marvel.loc.gov) which has keyword searching, allowing pursuit of documents for "foreign students" and "financial aid."

Since electronic education, or instruction via e-mail, is becoming available, and given the existence of worldwide cable television, one can imagine a not-too-distant advising future in which an adviser orients in regard to electronic and cable educational opportunities from the United States or other countries in the adviser's country.

COMMUNICATING TO ONE'S COMMUNITY

One of the most lamentable and frustrating dilemmas of advising is the following. If you walk across the campus of an American university and stop to chat with some foreign students, as an overseas adviser you are struck by the number who come to study in the United States yet never went to an advising center, and were not even aware of the existence of such offices. They came to the school they are attending based on the experience of a friend or relative, or on the recommendation of a colleague. When you ask them if they would have liked to know more of the process, or have had more options, they will often respond affirmatively.

At the same time, at the end of the day, advisers around the globe will be looking back over their day and its cases, thinking about the people with whom they spoke. For reasons of funding, language proficiency, or academic records, many will have no immediate chance of studying in the United States. Nevertheless, despite this lack of prospect, time was taken for their advising. On the one hand, therefore, are foreign students in U.S. colleges who would like to have received advising before coming to their current American school. On the other hand are individuals who went to an advising center and will have no immediate application for the information they received there.

This is the most tragic information gap in international education.

As you can imagine, a large part of the solution can be achieved by the overseas educational advising center. An advising center is not just an information service for those who come to it; it has to be a voice that reaches out to the community needing its service and not knowing about it.

Getting Messengers

Reaching out to one's community by visiting and lecturing can be a time-consuming and possibly self-defeating (time away from the center) chore for an adviser. However, there are many people who can efficiently, effectively, and widely send messages for you. Outreach programs for an adviser can sometimes best be done through the reach of others.

At the level of higher education, one of the most effective groups of communication contacts is the editors of local college and university newspapers and directors of campus radio stations. You can invite them to your center for a briefing session or a press conference. (Remember, if you work in a hierarchical situation—as most advisers do—be sure to get clearance at the right level for these kinds of meetings.)

Fundamental in the message you want conveyed are two things: what your service is and who will or will not benefit from it. You must emphasize that you are an advising center, a specialized library or information center, for study in the United States; you are not a grant-giving agency. This distinction should be repeated several times because the tendency will be to read into your message what people want to hear: financial aid for study abroad. Follow this emphasis with the qualifications for study: English proficiency, grades, and financing. Moreover, emphasize that the qualifications for a grant are more rigorous. Be sure to make these points at both the beginning and end of your meeting.

Such a meeting can be an annual or once-a-semester affair at your center.

You will also want to hold meetings at your center once a year with any educational advisers or international education personnel at local universities or higher education agencies. Administrators from local companies who direct parts of their personnel to study abroad may join these meetings.

At the secondary level, one also wants to meet annually with counselors at those private or public high schools most likely to have students wanting to participate in exchange programs. To identify these schools, a good relationship with the visa consul can be very helpful because that official can let you know from visa applications which high schools are sending the most students. The local representatives of exchange programs and of English language courses can also participate in this meeting.

All of these outreach "messengers" should be provided with copies of the appropriate handouts you give to advisees for their respective areas. They should receive a tour of your center, examining its resources. Moreover, they should know the important role they are carrying out in the effort to reduce the information gap in educational advising.

You as a Messenger

Obtaining and regularly orienting messengers is a powerful means of communicating the message of your center. You are multiplying your communication capacity better than videotape or photocopies and far more extensively than you could by yourself. They are your communication network in the community. The effectiveness of this network becomes apparent over several years as you and they become more accustomed to working with each other.

You can also produce a poster that announces your service. Your messengers should be amply supplied with these and asked to post them where they will be seen to best advantage. On an annual basis, these can be mailed, along with a posting request, to the central administration of all the schools, companies, and government agencies which should know about your service.

The annual meetings and mailings referred to above should be done as close to the beginning of the American academic year as possible. This and the next few months are the time when overseas students must be preparing applications for admission for the next academic year.

If you go outside the advising center to give talks about it, you should do so getting the maximum benefit out of this time. Maximum benefit means on the one hand delivering the briefing you earlier gave, that which repeats the basic points of your service without raising misconceptions. On the other hand, maximum benefit means giving that message to the right audience.

Education-related audiences are one's main interest. It is worthwhile to accept an invitation to speak at an education conference or give an interview for an education or public service radio or television program. Interviews for general audience radio or television talk shows can be disastrous, bringing in visits and

phone calls to an advising center by people who picked up only wishful messages.

In this chapter we have examined the most important stage of advising, communicating advising resources to advisees. We examined this communication in
the context of library reference service. Initially we concentrated on finding out
what information the advisee needed, focusing on interview techniques. Then
we examined how to respond to these needs, establishing the axis of the advising
environment through dialog and work between adviser and advisee. Finally we
considered methods by which an advising center can publicize its resources to
those in the community needing to know of them.

Having considered the gathering, organizing, and communicating of information, we will look in the next chapter at the management of information, the
maintenance of procedures and resources for advising.

5

Managing Information

In this book we have discussed how to acquire advising materials, how to arrange them for retrieval, and how to communicate their information. These resources (meaning the materials and the advisers, together with any support staff) and the activities related to them must be organized and maintained. This operation of organization and maintenance is known as management.

Management has already been part of our discussion. Collection development, the gathering and maintenance of library holdings, is also known as collection management. Maintenance of the library catalog is designated also as catalog management. This terminology goes far to show how much services which have information in the forefront require a great deal of management in the background.

However, the management for advising as a library or information service, which we will examine in this chapter, is different both in dimension and level. The previous dimensions of management have been for the procedures immediately related to advising: gathering, organizing, and communicating resources. Another dimension of management involves all the resources which keep the direct service of advising in operation, such as finances, professional and nonprofessional personnel, office space, and equipment, supplies, and furnishings. These resources support the core service operation, and their management forms the sustaining framework of an information service. It is this latter, wider dimension—the sustaining one—that we want to examine in this chapter. Since advising centers are invariably part of larger organizations, such as a foundation, cultural center, diplomatic post, or university, many of these latter aspects of management will wholly or in part be under the control of the host organization.

In addition to the sustaining aspect of management for advising, we want to examine two different levels of management for advising as an information service: library management and information management. The former refers to the managing of the advising center as an individual library administrative unit; the latter refers to the advising center as an information department for the larger organization or system of which it is a part.

In the first section of this chapter, therefore, we will look at the management of an advising center. Initially we will look at concepts of management and then examine the main units of management in advising. Thus we will examine the fundamental resource, the people or staff. From people we will go to places and things (that is, the office space and equipment in it). Next we will examine the record keeping necessary for staff, office, and equipment. Then we will focus on that aspect of management which underpins all the others, finances. Finally, we will consider evaluation, the analysis of performance and management.

Having examined the management of the advising center, we will then examine the information management function of a center. We will see how the advising center can aid the information needs of the organization or system of which it is a part. What does the larger entity need in terms of information? When and how does it need such information? We will see how to go about gathering that information and how to communicate or report it within the organization or system.

THINKING OF MANAGEMENT

Management as a field of study or intellectual discipline has received a great deal of attention in recent times. Numerous "schools" or approaches to it have emerged. We have seen the many ways in which advising involves management. As an advising center develops or as an adviser's career advances, it becomes increasingly important for an adviser to have a knowledge of management and an awareness of how to use and evaluate various approaches to it.

Management is a discipline which has been influenced by numerous others, particularly the social sciences, engineering, and mathematics. Within the social sciences, psychology, sociology, and economics have been particularly important. Each of these disciplines, as their influence has waxed or waned in management, has been responsible for the development of various schools or approaches.

Psychology has focused on management as primarily a matter of individual and interpersonal relations. Social psychology and sociology have emphasized it as human activity in groups. Economics has concentrated on rational choice and decision as the key aspect of management. From engineering has come a focus on the interaction of systems, human and technical. With mathematics there has been an emphasis on quantifying processes in management and thereby establishing it as a science.

As you can see, management actually involves wide interdisciplinary study. To depend on any one of the above disciplines as a tool for management is quite inadequate. To think of management as only interpersonal activities, as only humans and equipment organized together, or just as a sequence of correctly made rational decisions is ineffectively limited. However, management which encompasses the various perspectives which have contributed to it is a quite powerful tool of operation and evaluation, whether for an advising center, university library, auto factory, or international bank.

As an adviser managing a one-person center or one with a dozen staff and a nationwide public, you will always want to improve your skills in management. Numerous managing issues are relevant to you such as quality assessment, conflict resolution, or time management. The most productive and beneficial approach to management, however, is recognizing the various disciplines which incorporate it and absorb as much from them as you can through study, application, and experience. Thus you acquire the powerful, encompassing perspective which can make management so effective a discipline.

You can also better evaluate assessments made by managers or consultants of either your own or others' work to see how adequate or limited they are. For example, an office problem of conflict among numerous staff members may be interpreted by a manager with a psychology focus as a situation which requires change in individual behavior. However, someone with both this and a systems engineering perspective may perceive that the conflict is not due to personalities per se but to uneven levels of technical and professional competence among staff and of inadequate equipment. Dealing only with personalities in this case, therefore, will be ineffective until the root cause of conflict, uneven competence and technical inadequacies, is understood and resolved. The exclusively interpersonal interpretation could leave problems worse since focusing only on it may leave staff feeling intimidated about their character.

If you have a wide perspective in management, you will become more alert to the adequacy or inadequacy of organizational decisions. You will be able to analyze yourself, managers, and consultants in terms of limits or extent of managerial perspective. "The Management Theory Jungle Revisited" by Harold Koontz, long-time professor of management at the University of California, Los Angeles, is a concise and incisive article on the various perspectives of management, their adequacies and inadequacies.

MANAGING THE ADVISING CENTER AS A LIBRARY UNIT

Staff

The staff or people—meaning the advisers, any support staff, and possibly volunteers—are the key resource of an advising center. Assuming that advising is essentially a special library operation (before examining what an advising staff is or should be), it is important to understand an essential distinction about special library functions. This distinction is clearly made in Elin Christianson's *Special Libraries: A Guide for Management.* In this work special libraries are differentiated from public or university libraries in several respects. The emphasis of the special library is much more on a focused informational function rather than education, recreational reading, public interest, or academic research. Moreover, special libraries, rather than being separate entities, usually operate for and within an organization. Further, the subject of what they collect is limited in scope because they deal with a group of users with a limited and special interest. Finally, because of their focused and limited objectives, they are relatively small in terms of staff, collection, and space.

An advising office as a special library inherently will be small due to its focused group of users and collection limited to those user objectives. What then should be the size of an advising staff and, most importantly, what should be its composition?

Professional character of advisers. It is the assumption of this book that an adviser should be someone trained in one of the information professions: librarianship, information science, or information management. Because of the role of the librarian in developing a collection, acquiring materials, and organizing and communicating about them, a graduate in librarianship should be at the heart of the advising operation. The library training of this person should be rooted in information science—the computerized, electronic character of gathering and disseminating data which increasingly dominates contemporary and future information services.

A librarian operating in a special library has characteristics different from public or academic librarians. Out of the range of major activities for operating a library, the special librarian concentrates primarily on collection development and reference work. In conducting the latter service, the special librarian deals in a more direct and individual way with the user because of the specialized and focused nature of resources and research in the library resources.

If the adviser or principal member of an advising staff does not have a professional background in library and information science, then that person must be someone who has a demonstrated capacity to manage the functions of an information system as described in this guide.

Another underlying assumption about advisers is that they have at least an undergraduate university degree or diploma. This degree may be from the adviser's native country or wholly or in part from the United States or another country. At least some educational experience in the country about which advising is being done is as essential as having a professional information service background or capacity.

Size of advising center staff. Accepting this profile for an adviser, how many advisers or staff members does a center need? If an adviser carries out some of the administration and responsibilities previously described and has only limited audiovisual and computer aids, such an adviser should be able to deal with about 2,500 advising visits per year. This does not mean 2,500 advisees. Advisees visit a center once or many times. For 2,500 visits, an adviser will probably have less than a thousand advisees. On a daily basis, without any secretarial or clerical support staff, and with minimum equipment aids for advising and office routines, a full-time adviser can handle an average of ten advising visits per day, including both shorter and longer interviews. Full-time is calculated as eight hours per day, with three hours closed to the public for internal administration and five open to the public for advising.

A one-person advising center which is well supplied with advising and office equipment (that is, audiovisual, electronic, computer, and photocopying equipment) can handle fifteen and possibly up to twenty advising visits per day. The standard of how many advisees an adviser can handle per day is elastic depending upon support equipment. At a point where a single adviser's limits are met, it is necessary to have either more equipment or staff. If it is more staff, a secretary or clerk can be hired, possibly on a part-time basis. For administrative duties, this person relieves the adviser of having to prepare book orders, photocopy handouts, arrange bookshelves, or answer all phone calls.

However, by the time one adviser has to see twenty or more people per day, the strain becomes marked. When annual advising visits arrive at 5,000 per year, an adviser (even with a support staff person) will need at least another adviser on a part-time basis. Someone is needed, besides a secretary or clerk, who can take care of the intense work of dialog and research with advisees. A part-time adviser can initially serve to meet this increase.

The status of full or part-time will be determined by the amount of administrative and advisee support assistance the staff person can do, together with time-saving advising and the office equipment one has—and, of course, the adequacy of the budget. Regardless of these factors, however, it should be apparent that, whenever the public for an advising center grows by several thousand more visits per year, either another adviser or another support staff member (or a combination of these on a part-time basis) is needed.

When an adviser position becomes available, an announcement with a job description should be circulated. Figure 5.1 gives a suggested job description for a U.S. overseas educational adviser in a one-person operation. It describes what the adviser is expected to do and the background of training and experience desired to carry out the advising functions. The composition of job descriptions is usually done within the personnel or human resources department of the parent organization.

In a multimember center, the head of advising should be consulted about the announcement or asked to draft it. A committee should be established to examine candidate applications for the position and to interview selected ones. The advising center head should be part of this committee, ideally heading it.

Volunteers for an advising center. If funding does not allow even a part-time person to be hired, volunteers may be a way of solving staff shortage. Ideally volunteers are a short-term solution. Admittedly, in some American hospitals, museums, and libraries, volunteers have become a staffing staple, providing a steady, committed, and solid corps of workers. The fundamental concern in depending on volunteers is reliability. Time is required in training a volunteer

Figure 5.1
Job Description for Educational Adviser

Educational Advising Center

JOB DESCRIPTION
U.S. Overseas Educational Adviser
(Full-time Position)

Duties

The educational adviser gives information and orientation in English and local language for study and research in the United States. Advises for full spectrum of education, from preschool through elementary, secondary, and tertiary (undergraduate, graduate, and postdoctoral) levels. Advises also for English language and short-term course study. Provides information on topics ancillary to education such as financial aid, visas, adaptation to American culture and academic life, and readaption to native culture.

Acquires and or prepares printed, audiovisual, and electronic resources for advising. Organizes material for open access by advisees. Conducts advising on a group and individual basis. Maintains records of advising consultations and center activities and reports on same.

Qualifications

Must be university graduate, preferably in librarianship with emphasis on information science. Should have experience in collection development, reference service, and library or information center management. Should have at least one year of study in the United States, preferably at the tertiary level. Must have excellent spoken and written English. Should have ability to form wide, supportive network from among advisee, educational, diplomatic, professional, communications, and philanthropic sectors. Must have ability to establish and maintain cooperative activities with other advisers in country and region. Must have commitment to developing advising as professional information service.

Salary will be commensurate with experience; ample benefits provided. Candidates should send letter of application and resume together with addresses and phone numbers of three references to Educational Advising Center by 30 September 1994.

Note: This organization employs on an equal opportunity basis regardless of age, ethnic or national origin, gender, physical condition, race, religion, or sexual orientation.

either as an office assistant or an adviser. Without reliability both the training time and the extra aid are lost.

The IIE advising center in New York City, mentioned earlier, depends almost exclusively on volunteer advisers. They have helped tens of thousands of advisees. Two officials from IIE, Dulcie Schackman and Ed Battle, have written about this volunteer advising program in "The Three R's of Volunteers: Recruitment, Retention, Recognition" (*The Advising Quarterly* 17, Summer 1991, pp. 1, 5–7). They explain how to attract, keep, and reward volunteer advisers.

In this same issue, there is also an article by Marti Thomson, head of educational advising for the Fulbright Commission in Malaysia, "Establishing a Volunteer Advising Program" (pp. 1, 3–4) in which she explains how she organized her extensive program of volunteer advisers. She includes an outline of the materials used in her training packet for volunteer advisers (p. 8).

Staff management. Once an advising staff goes beyond one person, whether an adviser and a secretary or a head adviser, several other advisers, support staff members, and volunteers, staff management becomes paramount.

There are four essentials to such management: motivation, organization, information, and communication. Motivation concerns why a person is working, the monetary rewards, benefits, growth opportunities, and the chance to dominate a skill and be recognized for it. These aspects concern everyone on a staff from the director to a junior office assistant.

Organization concerns where and how a person works. At its heart is planning, developing objectives and the ways to meet them among or with part of a group. This process is dynamic, not a one-time affair placed on a piece of paper and occasionally, if at all, consulted. One must always be checking to see that means to the objectives are being carried out and evaluating whether the objectives have been met or were worth pursuing. Where and how people operate in an organization depend totally on the process of ongoing analysis and evaluation.

Information and communication are the momentum of this dynamic. For each member of a staff to meet objectives, whether designing a poster or advising for a short-term course in marketing, data or information and the communication of them are necessary. Data and information are changing; communication must be continuous. Like organization, information and communication deal with how one works. For organization, that "how" is dynamic. For the flow of information and communication, that "how" is its lubricant.

There should also be lateral integration of staff members. Each one should know how to do the duties of the person immediately above and below him or her in the office hierarchy. This integration facilitates staff awareness of the larger operation together with smooth operation in the absence of a staff member.

Staff conference. A key aid for maintaining the above components is regular staff conferences or meetings. (I prefer the word conference over meeting because the former emphasizes conferring or consulting among colleagues and the

latter indicates only physical encounter.) These conferences follow and underscore an office operation based on motivation, organization, information, and
communication.

The conference can begin by considering progress on current projects (old
business), which may include the status of ordering new catalogs, preparations
for a graduate engineering orientation program, or preparing an instruction sheet
for advisers on how to operate a newly-arrived compact disc reader. It is those
on the staff engaged in these projects who discuss them with the other members.

New projects (new business) are items under consideration. These may be
reorganizing some furniture or considering whether to get a second photocopier.
Depending on how the staff and the director consider the subject, it will or will
not become a project and enter into ongoing consideration in future conferences.

Another part of the agenda is for members to indicate any new information.
This may mean informing about a new visa consul, a new publication for advising undergraduates, or a change in hours for a financial aid agency. Insofar
as the advising center is part of a larger organization, the adviser in charge of
the center will regularly attend the appropriate division level staff conference or
meeting, reporting on advising activities during it and relaying to the advising
staff information from it.

Advising cases can also be discussed, especially those which highlight a need
for different or special treatment or a new way of dealing with advising procedures.

At the end of the conference, a summary or wrap-up should be made, especially of the main points of ongoing and new projects. This summary can be
given by the recorder. If conferences do not take place on a regular basis,
planning or announcement of the next one should be done. Special conferences
for certain projects or topics may also be announced. Advisers may want to
meet separately on a regular basis to focus solely on advising case analysis.

Figure 5.2 is an example of the notes from an advising center staff conference.
During the conference someone should be designated recorder, a duty that can
be done on a rotating basis among staff. The conference notes should be filed
for future reference regarding office and staff activities. Items for the agenda
can be suggested by any staff member. A note to other members indicating a
suggestion for the agenda can be circulated beforehand so that all can be prepared to consider it.

The value of the conference is not just for the impetus it gives to the work
of an advising center but also for its underscoring of the operating environment
of the center: consciousness of one's role and its integration with others, ongoing
checking and evaluation of work, continual communication of information and
data among staff, and integration of the advising staff with the information flow
of the host organization.

New adviser training. After advising, and possibly equal to it, the most important activity of an advising center is the training of a new adviser. The
importance of this activity is inherent to the advising process since the com-

Figure 5.2
Advising Staff Conference Notes

Current Projects
(or Old Business)
--*Ordering new catalogs. Half of form letters ready. Rest will be done by end of next week. Mailing in batches.*
--*Graduate engineering orientation program. Missing one panelist. Prof. One traveling. Other possibilities considered. Prof. Five will be contacted. Panel must be ready by next week when poster announcement prepared, which includes participants.*
--*Instruction sheet on new CD reader. Draft circulated. Drawing included to reinforce instructions. Final will be circulated tomorrow so that sheet can be ready by end of week, avoiding repeated questions from users.*

Information
--*New visa consul, Ms. I.M. Visas, arrives this week at U.S. Embassy. Head adviser will attend reception next week at which she will be present and invite to visit center.*
--*Hours of National Scholarship Board have changed for summer, operating from ten to five. Returns to regular schedule 10 September.*
--*Head adviser reported on host organization conference: new accountant appointed, Mr. I. T. Addsup; salary increase negotiations will continue until end of month; new tax withholding form must be filled out this week.*

New Projects
(or New Business)
--*Furniture reorganization in video room. Office assistants will prepare plan based on conference discussion and circulate to staff. Try to finalize next week.*
--*Acquiring second copier. Budget now can handle. Space major problem. Secretary will check market to see what smaller versions now available. Search will take week to ten days. Will report in two weeks.*

Advising Cases
--*Some advisees are misunderstanding parts of the new videotape on graduate study in U.S., thinking study plan means autobiography. Caused by problem of translation. Director will check to see if redubbing of part can be done. In meanwhile, check during first interview that point is clear to advisee.*

Wrap-up
--*New catalogs request letters finished next week.*
--*Prof. Five to be contacted for engineering program*
--*CD sheet ready by end of week.*
--*Furniture reorganization in video room will be circulating from office assistants.*
--*Secretary will indicate if smaller photocopier now available in two weeks.*
--*New graduate videotape needs redubbing for clarification of study plan preparation.*
--*Director will see if new visa consul can visit center.*
--*Summer hours at NSB, 10-5, until 10 September.*
--*New accountant, Mr. Addsup; tax form completed this week, new salaries by end of month.*
--*Next staff conference, next week, same day, same time.*

petence of an adviser establishes the value of the core service of an advising center.

Whether or not the new adviser is a librarian or information professional, a basic training program will be required. Advising sources are wide-ranging and highly specialized. The new adviser may be someone added to your staff or someone who is assuming responsibility at another center.

No adviser should take a position without having basic training provided, even if it requires that the hiring organization send the new adviser to another center for this training. This training should never be delayed. It should not occur after one begins advising. Basic training must occur and should only occur before an adviser ever sees an advisee.

It should be noted that USIA offers a U.S.-based adviser training program of several weeks duration during the spring of each year. This training program offers an excellent (even singular) experience of American education and culture. It is designed, like the MRB, for those who are part of the USIA-supported advising network. It does not, however, include everything appropriate for basic training, such as skills in acquisition and development of materials or advising communication techniques.

The basic training of an adviser has several phases, the first comprising introduction and reading. The introduction starts with a detailed tour of the advising center, seeing how its space is organized, the extent and location of materials and equipment, and how advisees move through and use the center. A new adviser should be provided with the College Board *Overseas Educational Advisers' Manual*, together with a copy of this guide as initial reading in adviser formation.

The next phase is training sessions on the content and use of materials for each of the academic areas and levels of advising. After these sessions, nonacademic topics, such as visas, predeparture and readaptation orientation, ethics, and interviewing techniques should be covered.

From this phase, the trainee can pass to observation of advising routines. The new advisee should observe advising cases in all areas and through all stages from general orientation and first interview through successive advisee research and later interviews. This observation phase should not be passive; the advising trainee should converse and inquire with advisees in order to get a sense of how they deal with resources and absorb information. Nevertheless, it may be the training adviser who answers most of the questions raised.

The final phase of adviser training is supervised advising, at first under intense then later less concentrated observation. During intense observation, the trainee conducts advising sessions but is always accompanied by the training adviser. In these circumstances advisees should not feel uncomfortable, but rather that they are being treated to two advisers. In the final phase too, depending on the administrative responsibilities of the new adviser, the person should receive instruction in advising center management routines.

Comment on each observed session by the training adviser should take place in private as soon after the session as possible. After advising sessions have been conducted in all areas, the trainee then can pass to partial observation, the trainer sitting in on occasional sessions.

Adviser Continuing Education. Not only basic training but also the continuing education or update training of advisers must occur. Workshops for this purpose can be planned by all the advisers in one country or a region of several countries. Advisers should try not to depend exclusively on outside agencies to organize these functions. A fundamental characteristic of professionals is organizing and providing their own conferences and workshops.

Outside agencies have a crucial role in providing funding. For this reason USIA, the local country USIS post, a Fulbright Commission, and international and local foundations should be invited to cooperatively fund an adviser conference. These meetings significantly improve advising, a service fundamental to their own operations.

Like basic training, conferences or workshops for updating the knowledge and skills of advisers are among the most valuable encounters they engage in. Advisers are communicators of information, and information constantly changes. These changes must be regularly communicated. The gathering of advisers to update themselves, absorb information changes, and maintain their continuing education is fundamental to the advising process.

The organization of a workshop takes time in terms of planning program content, panelists, conference location, participant accommodations, and reception and social events. The venue for workshops, therefore, should pass from one center or city in a country or region to another. On the one hand such mobility relieves any one center from always having the work of organizing the workshop. On the other hand, such mobility extends the experience and expertise of workshop organizing throughout the group of advisers. Thereby the occurrence of such meetings becomes less vulnerable due to lack of adviser knowledge or experience in conducting them.

The workshops also give a great deal of solidarity to a national or regional group of advisers. Everyone becomes familiar with the milieu in which others work. Since the axis of the advising environment is dialog and research, experiencing variations of the advising milieu allows one to expand and refine one's knowledge of operating environments. In addition, the workshop allows advisers to expand their professional network, permitting further contacts for facilitating advisee connections. Continuity to the workshop and to the maintenance of group effort can be obtained through publication of a newsletter and/or an e-mail network for the group.

Figure 5.3 is an example of a program for a regional advising workshop. It shows the various kinds of information which can comprise a workshop: visas, financial aid, study courses, computer uses, and professional practices. Through adviser committees, materials can be revised and group action taken on issues of importance. The committee work allows advisers not only to acquire new information during a workshop but to produce it from their own expertise.

Figure 5.3
Program for an Advising Workshop

IXth ANNUAL SOMEWHERE REGIONAL ADVISING WORKSHOP
Somewhere City, Country X
4-7 September 1994

Sunday
Arrivals during day. All participants staying at Somewhere City Grande Hotel, one block north of advising center. Program sessions will be held in hotel conference center and advising center.
7:00 p.m. Reception at home of U.S. cultural attache. Distribution of program packets.
Monday
8:30-10 Briefing and discussion on visas for study and research with visal consul from U.S. Embassy.
10:30-12:30 Briefing and discussion with panel of representatives from financial aid agencies.
2-4 Visit to host advising center. Examination of its resources, organization, and routines.
5-6 Organization of ad hoc adviser committees: 1) means of improving financing for educational advising, 2) revision of mission and goals statement. (Note: There should also be standing, or permanent, committees for such subjects as: planning and program of the next workshop, publications, computer resources, etc.)
7:30-9 Roundtable on advising cases.
(optional)
Tuesday
8:30-10 Briefing and discusson with local representatives of U.S. English language proficiency courses.
10:30-12 Briefing and discussion with local representatives of high school exchange programs.
1:30-3:30 Meeting of all ad hoc and standing committees.
4-5:30 Computer lab session on database development for advising.
7:30 Group dinner at Chez MacSomewhere Restaurant.
Wednesday
  Series of three practicums with guest faculty member:
8:30-9:30 1st Practicum: New electronic resources for advising.
9:45-10:45 2nd Practicum: Local production of advising materials.
11-12 3rd Practicum: Reference service techniques via e-mail.
1:30-2:30 Viewing of videotape (20 minutes), in production by USIA, on graduate medical study in U.S. Notes of discussion after viewing will be forwarded to Agency.
3-4:30 Presentation of committee reports.
4:30-5 Distribution and completion of workshop evaluations.
5:30 Closing remarks and reception (all panelists and guest participants invited). Departures.

Note how this workshop has been organized using advisers and local personnel as its main resources. Only one guest faculty member has been necessary and only for one day. Such local focus allows reduced cost in workshop organization and demonstrates the extent to which continuing education for advisers can be obtained from local resources.

Through both the formal and the social program of the workshop, contacts are expanded and professional interaction widened.

It should be noted that the general norm for duration of workshops or professional conferences is no more than three working days. If a fourth or fifth day is necessary, then the days of the weekend immediately preceding or succeeding the three are used. Five working days are not generally used so that participants do not "close" their profession from one weekend to another.

National and regional groups of advisers are also important for establishing coordinated acquisition of materials. Such coordination is fundamental to developing advising collections in as economical and useful a manner as possible.

Cooperative collection development among advisers can reduce costs and maximize use of materials. For example, reference works for advising can be quite expensive, sometimes over one hundred dollars per title. Among a group of advising centers in a national or regional organization, the cost of such items can be reduced by cooperative acquisition. Thus, rather than all members buying the same expensive title each year, half would do so one year, the other half the following year. All centers would then be updated for the current two years and, as needed, each could consult another for the most current edition. Works weeded from one collection could be circulated in a standard pattern to recipient centers.

The cost of compact discs can be alleviated by adviser organizations through computer networking. A project of this sort requires either the expertise of an adviser who has a systems or automation librarian background or consultation with such a professional. Rather than all centers buying the compact discs needed in advising, a "pyramid" of such resources can be established at one center with all others having access to it, a wide-area network (WAN). Each center contributes financially to the acquisitions. All centers thus have access to extensive electronic resources, but none has to pay for all of them. It should be noted, however, that the pricing of electronic resources rises in relation to the number of users who access them. Nonetheless, total advising center costs in cooperative acquisitions are still reduced despite this pricing practice.

For additional development as an information professional, an adviser should also think of joining the librarian or information professional association of the local country. The librarian association is often divided into sections for types of libraries. The sections for special libraries and for computerization of library and information operations can be excellent professional support and growth for an adviser. Through publications and meetings of the association, the adviser has access to experienced and innovative professionals and to continuing developments in collection development, reference service, and library management.

Mission and goals statement. We have seen that the heart of advising is the adviser working with an advisee. It should now be apparent that the success of that relationship is dependent very much on another—advisers meeting and working with each other. Out of that solidarity comes the professional enrichment which strengthens the adviser-advisee relationship.

A fundamental document for allowing coordinated action, among either the staff of an advising center or the advisers in a national or regional group, is a mission and goals statement. Through such a document, the center or the wider organization expresses two things. It first states its purpose, its all-embracing objective or mission. It then expresses the ways by which it intends to meet them. It indicates the goals that must be met in order to fulfill the mission.

As a section within a larger organization, the advising center should compose its mission and goals statement within the objectives of the host institution. This inclusion means preparing the advising statement in conjunction with or under its approval. The statement of a national or regional group can be made in a more autonomous manner.

Figure 5.4 shows an example of a mission and goals statement by an advising center which is part of a host organization. The center's mission is seen, therefore, in the context of that organization. The statement opens indicating the mission of the host organization and then follows by placing the mission of the advising center within that of the organization. The goals are those of the advising center. Although this statement was written by an advising center within a host organization, it could also serve for an independent office (admittedly, rare) or a national or regional organization of advisers. The modification for adaptation would be to the mission part of the statement rather than to the goals.

One of the principal objectives of the mission and goals statement is to achieve coordinated action in a staff or group. To this end, it is necessary that everyone who will be involved in carrying out the statement be involved in its composition. This means that all the members of a staff (or all advisers in a group) and all supervisory personnel for advising in a host organization should participate in its production.

A core of staff or members of a group may write a draft composition, but all should review, debate, and approve this for the final statement. Those who participate in its production must remember that they are writing not just for themselves but also for future members of a staff or group. The composers must have a sense of the long-term continuity and application of the statement, although later changes can and should be made. Once finished, the statement should be prominently displayed so that those who are committed to it and the advisees who are its objective can regularly view it.

Ethics. Not only mission and goals, but also ethics determine how one works in an advising center. While the former clarifies the abiding objectives of work, ethics indicate the moral principles which guide it. We have extensively examined the resources for advising, the environment for conducting it, and the formation of the adviser. And yet, what does any of this mean without ethics? All our marveling at instant electronic retrieval of information and its communication is meaningless—even dangerous—if there is not the possibility to trust the veracity of information and the character of its communication.

At the heart of ethics is integrity, the equilibrium between one's principles

Figure 5.4
Mission and Goals Statement

Educational Advising Center
of the Fellowship Foundation

Mission and Goals Statement

Mission

      The Educational Advising Center is a unit of the U.S.-Local Country Fellowship Foundation. The Foundation is a privately endowed, philanthropic organization, dedicated to maintaining friendship between the United States and this country. Such amity is pursued through financial support to local citizens for higher education, from undergraduate to postdoctoral levels, in the United States.

      The mission of the Educational Advising Center is to provide information regarding opportunities for study and research in U.S. higher education together with ancillary orientation necessary to that end. The Center serves as the educational information and orientation arm of the Foundation.

      The Center is open to all those in the community who wish to pursue American higher education regardless of whether they are candidates for grants from the Foundation, from other agencies, or are self-financed.

Goals

      To accomplish its mission, the Center has established the following goals:

      1. Human Resources. The adviser is recognized as the main resource for advising. This person must be a graduate information professional with basic training in U.S. educational advising and regular courses of continuing education. The primary activity of the adviser is to maintain dialogue and accompany research with advisees pursuing U.S. higher education opportunities. This activity is done with an attitude of support which leads to self-reliance on the part of the advisee. In relation to the primary activity, advising, the adviser manages the human and other resources of the Center. Additional advising and support staff are provided as proven necessary.

      2. Research Resources. The resources for research about opportunities in American higher education, and ancillary processes to this objective, are as current and extensive as possible. They comprise all types of resources from printed to audiovisual and electronic. All resources are organized for public access by advisees.

      3. Physical Resources. The Center maintains an open yet confidential environment in which advisees can research and interact with advisers. It is open at days and hours accessible for advisees with varying schedules. It provides support items for research such as worksheets and photocopying. Since the Center is not a publicly-financed service, it charges a registration fee equivalent to one hourly minimum wage, which is valid for one year.

and one's practice of them. The integrity of an adviser is a value which penetrates throughout the advising process.

Because of that integrity, an advisee can have confidence in the reliability of the advising sources used; the advisee can trust the orientation and guidance of the adviser and feel safe to discuss confidential matters; and advisers can confer among each other with security and for authentic development.

All misrepresentation of advising expertise erodes the advisee's ability to trust the resources used, orientation given, and confidentiality for it. It undermines the confidence of advisers to cooperate and develop with each other.

In advising, as in any professional service, ethics is the coin of the realm. Without integrity, the character of information, guidance, confidentiality, and cooperation disintegrate under the cancer of misrepresentation.

For advisers who are members of NAFSA, OSEAS' 1988 "Code of Ethics for Overseas Educational Advisers" is reprinted in Appendix C. NAFSA has a Committee on Ethical Practice to which members can have recourse for violations of ethics.

Space and Equipment

Space. Having looked at advisers and advising staff, who they are and how they act, let us now see where these people work. The organization and layout of an advising center is something over which an adviser will have only relative control. However, an adviser may obtain more control over organization and layout of space as improvements to a center have to be made or as one has the opportunity to remodel or establish a new advising center. For such activities, principles of advising space organization should be kept in mind.

Insofar as form follows function, and as style reflects substance, one does not begin designing an advising center by thinking of desks, computers, bookshelves, plants, and so on. One first thinks of what advising space is used for, and then what to put in it and how to arrange it to satisfy those objectives.

An advising center is a special library or information center with resources for study or research in the United States or another country. It is staffed by information professionals who are specialists in the acquisition of these resources and the communication of their use. Users have open access to the advising materials and professionals.

Because of these characteristics, advising centers have clusters or nodes of activities that are common to each of them. Information is available in a library area containing advising materials, and they are accessible by advisees. Communication regarding needs and materials occurs both generally and individually (or privately) so that there are appropriate areas for each type of communication.

Figure 5.5 shows advising center space laid out along the above principles. Both small and large spaces are shown, emphasizing the relevance of these principles to any size center. All have the same basic clusters or nodes of activities. Only activities of reception, storage, and staff work space become more prominent spatially as an advising center has a larger public, resources, and specialized staff; and these activities are related to administration rather than the core advising service.

Out of the functions of an advising center, one can not only perceive principles for the organization of its space but, moreover, for its decor. The manner of expressing this decor will, admittedly, vary depending on personal and cultural taste.

One principle of decor should be receptivity or warmth, reinforcing the fact that advisees are welcome to use materials and consult with advisers. Ultimately it is the adviser and any staff who are the substance of such receptivity or warmth. Nevertheless, a decor of warmth underscores this: a natural environment of light and plants, carpeting which subdues sound, neutral or soft colors, wood as opposed to metal, and so on. These elements may not transfer, though, across all cultures or tastes as "warmth"; some of the elements may say "boring" or "bland." Nevertheless, the principle of receptivity is relevant. Its stylistic expression changes, of course, depending on individual or cultural tastes and assumptions.

A dignified or decorous atmosphere can be considered another principle for advising decor. This principle expresses the priority of the environment for research and professional consultation. It discourages chatting or group diversion. The elements of an environment which especially underscore dignity and decorum are orderliness and cleanliness. Staff manner here, too, is fundamental. However, given the youthful environment of an advising center, no one will want these principles to result in a heavy or stodgy ambience.

Besides warmth and dignity, a modern decor is also appropriate. Advising is information, communication. It must be current; it must be open. A modern decor helps to send such a message. Nevertheless, it is but style, not substance. Only if advising materials and equipment are current and ample, if advisers are easily available, does the modern decor send a true message.

One may disagree with the above principles of decor. Some may say, for example, they prefer a traditional environment rather than a modern one. The former can better underscore the authority and reliability of information. Such things can and should be discussed.

The important thing is that one understand the decor of an advising center as being based on principles, like the layout of space, arising from the functions of the center. Style reflects substance; form follows function. Unless these principles and their expression are understood, a misleading message may be sent, creating an atmosphere contrary to the advising environment.

Equipment. The equipment an advising center needs is determined by its core advising operation and/or supporting administrative one. One can use photocopiers; video, audiocassette, and compact disc players; computers; printers; typewriters or word processors; filing cabinets; phone answering and fax machines; security alarms against theft of materials; maybe even a vacuum cleaner. Which of these do you need for either or both of your advising and administrative

Figure 5.5
Principles for Advising Space

The principal activities which occur in an advising center
are communication and research. Communication is both
general and private. Space, therefore, should reflect
these objectives: general communication, private
communication, and research. Based on these principles,
one can plan for any shape of office space or size of
advising staff and accommodate advising center needs.

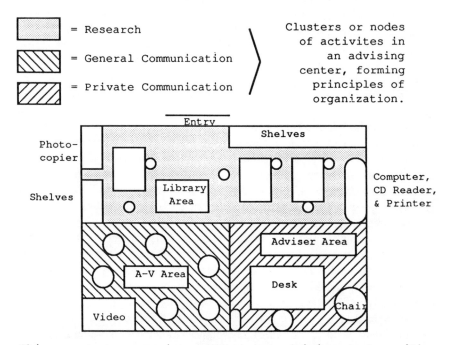

This one-room space is a one-person advising center with
areas separated by dividers or screens. The public
enters via the research area. The private area in the
lower right has the adviser's desk and a chair for
private consultation with an advisee. This place is
divided from the research area and the general
communication area by screens, allowing privacy. The
adviser's desk is situated to allow seeing into the
research area and towards the entry. The general
communication area is also separated by a screen from the
research area. Any sound projecting equipment, such as
from video, would be placed in the lower left corner to
least inconvenience others in the center.

Figure 5.5 (continued)

A larger space can be designed along the same principles.

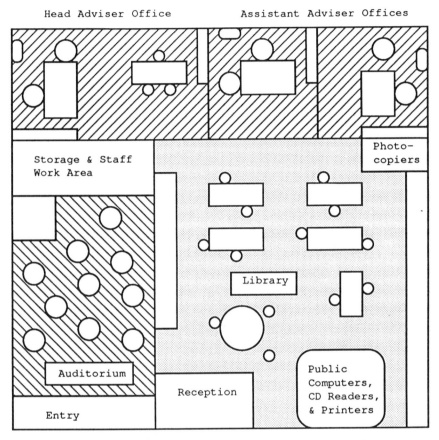

As advising space enlarges in response to increased public and staff, ancillary nodes to the principal ones emerge, such as reception, storage, and staff work area.

operations? What are the priorities for acquisition? What is the funding for purchases?

Should you get a computer or a word processor before a photocopier? Both pieces of equipment serve your two operations. But can you do much on the former before you have the latter? If you get a computer and a printer, how much later can you get the photocopier?

These questions emphasize that an adviser needs to determine what pieces of equipment are needed over the short and long term and prioritize how they will be acquired. To do this requires being continuously aware of what is on the market and at what price. The latest catalogs of library and office equipment supply companies must be part of the library. Perusing these can not only be tantalizing, but also educational. There are items in them one never imagined existed for dealing with a library public or maintaining an office operation.

Among the network of contacts an adviser establishes (rather ample as we have seen by now), those with library and office equipment salespeople are important. The more you are known for equipment and supplies sought and bought, the more you obtain discounts and alerts about new items available.

For the preservation of equipment and supplies, it is important to recall how heat, light, and/or moisture activate the deterioration of physical materials. The volatility of materials to these factors is relative. Those that are most sensitive, such as tapes, microfiche, slides, compact discs, and similar items, need to be appropriately stored.

Records

An advising center's records should be both quantitative and descriptive. Statistics should indicate both the total number and the numeric profile of the advising public. Reports should describe the activities developed and maintained by the center.

Statistics. Statistics are the numeric record of the growth and changing nature of the advising public. They are important in order to know how and when to respond objectively to a growing public with more staff and resources and how to respond to a changing public with different materials. Their data is also important for objectively showing appropriate supervisory personnel what the amount and character of your advising work has been. Figure 5.6 is an example of a statistics sheet for an advising center. One obtains the data for this sheet from the advisee data record (Figure 4.1). Every time a new advisee fills out a data record or one is pulled from the file for an advisee's visit, an accumulation of records is left by the end of the day from which the statistics record can be made. The period by which one keeps statistics (the week or the month) varies depending to some extent on the size of a center and how closely one is trying to follow the changing growth or profile of a public.

Advising center statistics present themselves as excellent candidates for a computer database or spreadsheet. One can thereby more precisely compare variables and perceive trends. Which types of advisees have more deficiency in English? Are more likely to need financial aid? Which form of the media has most divulged information on the center to graduate business advisees? Is there a changing gender balance in those who are seeking high school exchange programs? What is the average number of visits for an undergraduate advisee? Does the number vary by gender? By type of financing?

Reports. Statistics will be an element to incorporate into reports describing your advising activities. Descriptive reports can be annual, every three or four months, or monthly. Their frequency is generally determined by the supervisory

Figure 5.6
Advising Center Statistics Sheet

Educational Advising Center
Statistics of Advising Visits

Week of (or Month of) _____   Total

Higher Education

Undergraduate	First Visit	_____
	Further Visits	_____

Graduate	First Visit	_____
	Further Visits	_____

Areas of Specialization

Funding
Personal   _____

Financial Aid   _____

Other Study
English Courses   _____

High School Exchange   _____

Short-term Study   _____

How Found out about Service
Advisee   _____

At School   _____

At Work   _____

From Newspaper   Radio   Television   _____

Gender	**Age Group**	
Male	Pre-teen	20-25
Female	Teenager	25-30
		+30

Total of All Visits
(Higher Education and Other Study) _____

personnel for whom they are prepared. A combination of reporting, based on an annual report together with reports at some regular interval of months, can allow focusing on trends for the annual report and on data and activities in the latter type. The months-based reports can give more substance to what the annual report eventually describes.

A suggested format for reporting can be seen in Figure 5.7. This example shows only the outline of the report; the topics listed need to be described. Each entry within a section can consist of one or two paragraphs. Reporting is very important for the financing of advising, proving what has been well spent and showing what should continue to be supported.

Inventory. The parent organization is generally responsible for maintaining inventory, overseeing the acquisition and retirement of items, and keeping the inventory catalog record. The advising center should have a copy of those records which pertain to it. This local record is a benefit to both the organization and the center, allowing each to maintain a check of items. One can check inventory against these records once a year, possibly at the time weeding is done.

Inventory records may be maintained on cards or as a database. They are generally organized by the keyword of the item, such as, ''chair, swivel,'' ''computer, personal,'' or ''table, conference.'' With this are included brand name, model, serial number, and price. The host organization adds an accession number which, for control purposes, appears on both the inventory record and the item itself.

Financing of Advising

Funds for advising can be seen from two perspectives; the amount which is needed for its conduct and provided by a host agency, and that which an advising center can attempt to raise.

What is needed. As a unit within a larger organization, the advising center has its budget calculated by that entity. At best, therefore, all an adviser can do is indicate what is needed. As in most libraries, an advising center will have needs in three principal areas: staff, research materials, and related costs.

Most organizations estimate the budget of the coming year based on the current or immediate past budget. These budgets are estimated for a fiscal year, a period which is often different from the calendar or academic year. Therefore, an adviser must always calculate financial resources in relation to various perspectives. Moreover, an advising center may be expanding but the finances of the parent agency either growing or contracting. The budget suggestions of an adviser must therefore be ready to move in several directions: to expand, to protect the status quo, or to prioritize for strategic reductions.

There is usually a scheduled time before the beginning of the fiscal year when the next budget is prepared. The adviser, either through a regular or special

Figure 5.7
Report Format

Educational Advising Center
Four-Month Report
January-April, 1994

A. Statistics on Advising Public
    1. Graph
    2. Profile of Users
    3. Analysis

B. Meetings and Visits
    1. Student Newspaper Editors
    2. Foreign Student Adviser from X College in New York
    3. Local High School Exchange Program Representatives
    4. Director of X English Course in California
    5. Mayor's Assistant for International Affairs

C. Programs
    1. Predeparture Orientation Program
    2. Training of Two Part-Time Volunteer Advisers
    3. Regional Advising Workshop Preparations

D. Projects
    1. Preparation of New Brochure on Student Visas
    2. Production of Videotape on MBA Study in U.S.
    3. Results of Survey on Advising Materials

E. Administration
    1. New Office Assistant
    2. Database on Advisee Consultations
    3. Theft of an Advisee's Briefcase
    4. Complaints Regarding Inadequacy of Photocopiers

report or a memo, should present a suggested budget. It is very important in presenting an operating budget, one which itemizes the cost of operating for one year, to link it to performance. The performance statements for an operating budget reinforce with specific details how funds will improve or economize an operation. Reports one previously submitted, giving advisee data and activities descriptions for a center, become crucial at the time of budget preparation. They demonstrate what has been well spent, what should be financed for further expansion, or what should be preserved in times of retraction. Figure 5.8 shows an operating budget with performance implications.

Some organizations may not request that individual units make budget suggestions. While formal presentation, therefore, cannot be made, the adviser should make use of informal professional and social opportunities to show what

Figure 5.8
Operating Budget with Performance Notations

Educational Advising Center
Suggested Operating Budget

A. Staff
    1. Adviser (full-time)   _____
    2. Secretary (two-thirds time)   _____
    3. Volunteers (no salary)
                                            Total _____
B. Advising Materials and Equipment
    1. Books (individual orders)   _____
    2. Vendor plan renewal   _____
    3. Nonbook materials (audio-
        visual and electronic)   _____
    4. CD Reader and printer   _____
                                            Total _____
C. Additional Costs
    1. Supplies and postage   _____
    2. New word processor   _____
    3. Equipment maintenance
        contracts   _____
    4. Noncontract repair costs   _____
    5. Adviser travel   _____
    6. Outside printing   _____
    7. Social expenses for
        programs   _____
                                            Total _____

            TOTAL OPERATING COSTS _____

Item A.3 economizes x amount in costs through volunteer
service for advising and administrative support work.
Additional staff is needed to serve the advising public
which has increased by 26 percent in the past year (see
last annual report presented by advising center).

Item B.2 includes a 10 percent discount on all purchases,
saving x amount and allowing more individual book orders.

Item C.2 will allow the secretary and volunteers to be more
efficient in preparing publications which the center
produces.

Item C.3 has given lower costs for repairs and allowed
longer life to equipment due to regular maintenance.

advising needs and what the benefits to the organization will be. The "wish list" referred to in Chapter 2 has reached its moment to be delivered.

Income from advising. If a parent organization allows its units to generate income, the advising center can consider ways to do this for its benefit and that of the organization. It is unlikely that a center can generate sufficient income to cover its costs, but it can defray some of them for the parent organization.

As the advising center shows not just educational and social benefits for the parent organization but also financial ones, its weight is improved in both the public administrative and private political contexts. As an advising center may thereby improve its position within an organization, it is important at this point to observe that individuals and human groups are political, engaged in acquisition of power and decision over their domain and interests.

To a greater or lesser extent, political agendas are always beneath any other more public ones. The adviser must be prepared to recognize the extent of a political environment and operate in it. The latter often has the greater weight on administrative decisions than the former per se.

Advising does not have many ways to raise income, and those which it has have caused controversy among some. One way is through charging for advising. While charging for all services can be needlessly complicated and prejudicial to needy students, there can be an annual registration fee, based on a local standard of affordability by the average student.

State universities and public libraries are funded by taxes. Special libraries are private entities and do not have this base, therefore often charging a membership fee. If some advisees may not seek the service because they cannot afford it then conditions can be established for waiving a fee.

An advising center can also charge for the orientation programs (predeparture, graduate engineering, MBA, etc.) it stages for the public. Charging for photocopiers and printers in advising centers can also be a source of income.

Some in advising feel uncomfortable about any charging. To me it seems unrealistic to allow advisees to believe that advising is "free," especially when at private (or even some public) universities they may be paying a library and/or computer lab fee and paying also for photocopying and computer paper. If advisers enroll in a seminar for learning some new technique, they expect to pay a fee. Advising is a private seminar for learning a complex series of techniques.

The most convincing argument for advising to assume responsibility for generating income is the benefit this gives advising. Electronic information resources and equipment are expensive, much more so than books as resources. For advising centers to fulfill their commitment to having the most current and ample resources, they must generate (at least partially) the income to cover the high cost of these resources.

Evaluation

Having looked at the many components which comprise management in an advising center, from staff to space, records, and finances, we must examine the evaluation of advising. It will comprise evaluating the staff, the head adviser, and the advising center.

Staff evaluation. If you are an adviser who heads a staff of one other or many members, you will have the responsibility of evaluating the work performance of these individuals. These can be nervous annual encounters in which the evaluator and the evaluated are anxious about whether the right conclusion is being arrived at, and how cataclysmic a wrong one might be. However, in a communicative managerial environment, this tension need not occur if a supervisor habitually gives evaluative comments of support or for improvement throughout the year—and such evaluation even becomes an example of communication among employees.

Systems and procedures for evaluation differ. An adviser may have to follow a set of annual procedures determined by the host organization for employee evaluation. One of the most important things about evaluation is that work performance goals be understood equally between evaluator and evaluated. The latter must have as much opportunity as the evaluator, either orally or in writing, to express how goals have been fulfilled.

If one's host organization does not have a regular employee evaluation procedure, the adviser should consider establishing one in the center. At the beginning of a person's employment or of working with an individual, the adviser should review the job description in detail with the person. If there is an expectation that the employee grow beyond this job profile, what this means should be detailed.

On an annual basis the employee can present a report or essay on how he or she has met goals. This report should be presented to the adviser, who reviews it, prepares comments, and discusses it with the employee together with the adviser's report. All of this documentation and discussion should become part of the evaluation record, together with recommendations for continuation, promotion, or termination.

The importance of respectful frankness in evaluation interviews cannot be underestimated. The ways in which goals have or have not been met should be objectively shown, itemizing specific accomplishments or deficiencies. Politeness should never allow one to avoid frankness. A deficiency ignored comes to be regarded as conduct allowed. It grows and its correction becomes more difficult as much because it is now more extensive as because it has become understood as permissible.

Head adviser and advising center. The adviser, as a unit head in an organization, is responsible for evaluating the advising staff. Evaluation of the head adviser occurs by the appropriate supervisor. It is most important, if a person outside advising is evaluating an adviser, that supervisors know what advising involves. The key documents for such individuals to have, if not already familiar with them, are the mission and goals statement, the head adviser's job description, and advising center reports. The head adviser may even volunteer to write a report on what he or she considers to have been their performance during the year, much as the adviser received advising staff reports.

The evaluation of the head adviser is one thing; it analyzes the performance of an individual. Evaluation of the advising center, a service operation, is a separate matter. Some organizations may think that in evaluating the head of a unit the unit itself is also evaluated; that is to confuse the baker with the bakery.

If the organization does not evaluate the service per se, the adviser may consider how to do this. Having such analysis is of singular value; it allows one to work more clearly. One can see and be satisfied with what is going well. One can determine where deficiencies are and focus attention on them.

The user survey examined in Figure 2.2 can also serve in obtaining an evaluation of the advising center in terms of its core service. The questionnaire for the evaluation survey can be designed along one's mission and goals statement. Thus the questions of the survey can link the center with the purpose for which it is operating.

Evaluation is the last step in considering the management of an advising center as a library or information center unit within an organization. However, the advising center can also be considered as a unit gathering and distributing information for the organization itself. As a library unit, the advising center has an external function—its main one—gathering and communicating information to advisees. As an information service for the organization, it has an internal function of gathering and distributing data in accord with the information requirements of the organization. This internal operation is known as information management.

INFORMATION MANAGEMENT

In the information age it has become increasingly apparent that just as organizations need capital, labor, and equipment in order to function, so too they need information. Consequently, to the finance, personnel, and systems managers companies have added the information manager. The role of the information management unit in an organization is to gather and distribute data and information within that organization so that the right decisions are made for such things as pricing, warehousing, energy expenditures, and so on. It is a crucial element for production and planning.

An advising center is a special library or information center maintained by an organization for an advising public. An advising center is not the information management unit of the organization, but the center deals with data that can make it have information management functions for a host organization. In carrying out these partial functions, it can more fully serve and incorporate itself into the operation of the host organization. In the capacity of carrying out information management functions, the advising center obtains, analyzes, and routes information to the administration of the organization.

For example, let us assume that an advising center operates as a unit within a binational cultural center. The center maintains an extensive educational program of English courses, its mainstay for income. The advising center notes the number of advisees who wish to study English in the United States. It even notes that many want to study business English. However, almost all of them do not have the financial resources to do so.

This data is an important pattern of information for the host organization. It shows demand for a product (business English) which the organization may be able to provide. The advising center, in its role as an internal information unit, routes what is has perceived to the administration, initiating an information flow through the organization. Upon receiving this information, the administration can study it in conjunction with the English courses department and examine the feasibility of setting up a business English course, together with its profitability.

Consider another example, this time one in which an advising center operates as part of an organization for educational exchange between the United States and another country, such as a Fulbright Commission. The advising center may note a high number of artists, actors, dancers, painters, and ballet dancers seeking study or training opportunities in the United States. However, few agencies are offering financial aid for such study.

At the same time the adviser knows that the host organization is looking for ways to make its program a unique contribution to local needs, offering opportunities that other agencies do not. Therefore, the adviser can route to the administration the information about unmet artists' needs. This information can then be considered for its viability and relevance.

An advising center functions principally as an information service for an external public. However, through its data gathering and analysis, it notes information which can have an internal application, something useful for the host organization, aiding production, profitability, and/or planning. Gathering, analyzing, and distributing information for internal organizational use is an information management function that an advising center can carry out. Figure 5.9 shows such an information management flow, initiated by an advising center. Carrying out such functions does not mean that the advising center is an (or the) information management unit of an organization. Its inherent purpose is not this focus but rather serving an external advising public.

An important element in the flow of information generated by an advising center is that the administration, after deliberating and deciding, respond to the center. The response should indicate what the decision process has been. This response is as important to the center as to the institution because it will allow the former to gather data in a more focused and efficient manner for the latter. This cycle of advising initiated input and administrative output (or not), together with feedback to the center, is the heart of the flow in an information management process.

Figure 5.9
Information Management Flow

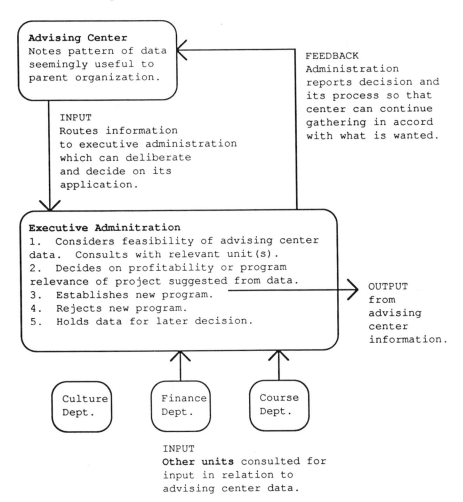

In this chapter we examined managing the advising center as a library unit and also as an internal unit with information management functions. The advising center is primarily an external information service, and we concentrated on examining its management of staff, space and equipment, record keeping, financing, and evaluation.

This management of information was the last stage in the information continuum described at the beginning of this work. We began with gathering information, then proceeded to organizing, and finally to communicating it. With this chapter, therefore, this guide to establishing advising centers as professional information centers comes to its end—and your work begins.

Conclusion

I am attempting to think what readers may say as they come to the end of this book.

"How much detail there is in advising. I never imagined!"

"There's too much here. I haven't the time or the funds for all of this."

"Well, really. How surprising. He forgot such-and-such!"

"At least now I've got a better idea of what's involved in advising, and I think I can go about it a bit more systematically."

The first comment is probably what I would have said, were I reading this work some years ago as a new adviser. I might have said the second too, except that as the author I know how much of librarianship and information science I have left out as not applicable to or feasible in advising: automation, circulation, preservation, to name a few. The third comment I expect. The last one I hope for.

From my own perspective, not as the author but as an experienced adviser, my own comment would be, "Oh, how I wish there had been something like this when I began."

The amount of details involved in applying library and information science to overseas advising may indeed seem overwhelming. What seems normal to an experienced librarian may seem overwhelming to a novice. If, however, you are convinced that the essential professional development needed for advising is to refine it as an information service, you have here the basics for beginning that refinement.

One of the most important things I hope you will have absorbed from this book is a sense of the continuum and flow of the information system: gathering, organizing, communicating, and managing information. Recognizing the relevance of this for advising, you progressively can begin to absorb the details of collection development, cataloging, reference service, and library and information management.

The conclusion I make about this book, and I believe you will eventually, is not that it is enough or that it is too much. It is too little. More is needed. Once you have learned and applied the basic aspects of library and information science explained here, I am sure that you as an adviser will want to know more of these disciplines. From that perception, I hope that this book ultimately persuades advisers to enroll in a degree or certificate program of library and information science or information systems and management. From this cadre will come the pioneer information professionals of advising. Toward that end, may this book have served as a catalyst.

Obtaining the degree or certificate of a librarian, information manager, or other information specialist can be a bountifully rewarding step in professional development. Who knows but that you may even join the international student legions yourself and come to the United States or go to another country for such study. Having managed an advising service as a special library or information center, you can move on in your career to other special library or information management positions, which often are in the private sector and offer competitive salaries. If you remain in advising, you will be one of the cadre I mentioned above. Within OSEAS and other advising associations, librarians should organize themselves as a section to concentrate and propagate their fundamental expertise for advising.

In closing, I reiterate what has been the basic principle and motivation for writing this book. An increasing characteristic of the international future will be the desire—indeed, the need—of studying in another country. International educational advising must therefore be prepared, developing itself as a professional information service to meet this crucial requirement of the emerging world community.

There is a Chinese proverb that tells us a journey of a thousand miles begins with the first step. Your career as an adviser begins with your opening words to your first advisee; it will last until your final recollection of all the advising cases that followed. It will endure in advising as long as your words are remembered by your advisees and passed on by them to others.

The Adviser

is now .

Appendix A

List of Titles in Minimum Reference Bookshelf (MRB) and Select Reference Collection (SRC)* as of 1993

Accredited Institutions of Postsecondary Education: Programs, Candidates

Adviser's Manual of Federal Regulations Affecting Foreign Students and Scholars

The Advising Quarterly

Allied Health Education Directory

"Arrival Information Requests"

The College Handbook, Index of Majors, and *Foreign Student Supplement**

A Comparative Guide to American Colleges: For Students, Parents, and Counselors

Directory of Accredited Home Study Schools

Directory of Engineering and Engineering Technology: Undergraduate Programs

*Directory of Overseas Educational Advising Centers**

Directory of Private Accredited Career Colleges and Schools

Diversity, Accessibility, and Quality: A Brief Introduction to American Education for Non-Americans

The Doctor of Philosophy Degree

Engineering College Research and Graduate Study

*English Language and Orientation Programs in the United States**

Foreign Teaching Assistants in U.S. Universities

Funding for U.S. Study: A Guide for Foreign Nationals

Graduate Medical Education Programs

Handbook of Private Schools: An Annual Descriptive Survey of Independent Education

The HEP Higher Education Directory

Lovejoy's College Guide

NAFSA Directory

NAFSA Newsletter

1991 ABET [Accreditation Board for Engineering and Technology] Accredited Yearbook

Occupational Outlook Handbook

The Official Guide to MBA Programs

Open Doors: Report on International Educational Exchange

Overseas Educational Advisers' Manual*

Peterson's Annual Guides to Graduate Study*

Peterson's Annual Guides to Undergraduate Study*

Profiles: Detailed Analysis of the Foreign Student in the United States

"Request for Application Materials from U.S. Colleges and Universities"

Appendix B

Multinational Educational Advising Materials

This book has concentrated on materials for advisers orienting about American education. However, many advisers in international education orient for the United States and/or several other countries. I observed at the beginning of this book that I would like to see future guides for advising in international education supplement this one by describing the educational orientation materials of other countries. In an effort to begin that supplementary work, there follows a list of a few education information resources for some of the countries sought in international education. Several of these sources are oriented toward a U.S. readership; nonetheless, they are useful for other nationalities.

WORLD

For higher education and financial aid:

International Handbook of Universities. Paris: International Association of Universities, 1993. Lists universities of the world by country, including addresses and communication numbers. Gives divisions of the universities and names of some officials. The International Association of Universities also publishes biennially a more concise directory on the same topic, entitled the *World List of Universities.*
Study Abroad-Études à l'étranger-Estudios en el extranjero, XXVIII. Paris: UNESCO, 1993. Directory of financial aid and course information for higher education in most countries of the world. Organized by countries, the work has an introduction for each entry with a section, "information service." This section details agencies which provide further information on financial aid, study, or research in that country. Because of such information, this publication is a unique guide to global sources of information on educational advising. Entries are in English, French, or Spanish.
Vademecum to University Reception-Vademecum d'accueil universitaire. Verona, Italy: Edizioni Futuro, 1989. Six-volume work, produced by the Council of Europe,

with text in English and French. The volumes respectively cover study in universities of the following countries: (1) Germany (western), (2) France, (3) Italy, including the Vatican and San Marino, (4) the Netherlands and Belgium, (5) Spain and Greece, and (6) the United Kingdom and Ireland.

Work, Study, Travel Abroad: The Whole World Handbook. New York: St. Martin's Press, 1994. Gives not only study and financial aid information for most countries of the world but includes information on work and travel opportunities and related regulations.

The World of Learning, 1994. London: Europa Publications, 1994. Lists by country the universities, research centers, libraries, and archives of the world, giving addresses and communication numbers.

There are also discipline-specific world guides such as *The Schirmer Guide to Schools of Music and Conservatories throughout the World*, the *World Directory of Dental Schools*, or the *World Veterinary Directory*. The German publisher Wolfgang Saur produces many world directories, including ones for libraries, archives, research centers, and museums.

AUSTRIA

For higher education:

Koller, Ludwig. "University Extension Courses at Austrian Institutions of Higher Education." Vienna: Austrian Foreign Student Service (AFSS), 1987. Courses listed by fields of study and then by universities offering. Entries include information on admission, course duration, tuition, and university address.

Koller, Ludwig, and Christine Anderle. *Information for Foreign Students to Study in an Austrian Institution of Higher Education.* Vienna: AFSS, 1990. Explains Austrian system of higher education and method for admission. Gives cost and addresses of universities together with admission advisers. Includes table indicating fields of study and universities offering them.

For language study:

Koller, Ludwig. "German Language Courses for Foreign Applicants and Students in Austria." Vienna: AFSS, 1989.

For study and research information:

AFSS
University of Vienna
Dr. Karl-Lueger-Ring 1
A-1010 Vienna, Austria

CANADA

For higher education and financial aid:

Many guides to U.S. colleges and universities, cited in Chapter 2 of this book, also include Canadian institutions, such as the *Peterson's Annual Guides* for undergraduate and graduate study, *Barron's Profiles, The College Blue Book*, etc. In addition, many discipline-specific publications for the United States, such as *The Directory of M.A. and Ph.D. Programs in Art and Art History* (New York: College Art Association, 1992) or the *Dance Magazine College Guide: 1992–93* (New York, Dance Magazine, Inc., 1992) include Canadian institutions.

For language study:

Conseil des programmes de langues secondes au Canada = Council of Second Language Programs in Canada. Brochure = Directory. [Ottawa]: Conseil . . . = Council . . . , n.d. Full-page description, with color photos, of English and French language courses in Canada.

FRANCE

For higher education and financial aid:

Centre national des oeuvres universitaires et scolaires (CNOUS). *Je vais en France, 1993: guide a l'intention des etudiants étrangers.* Paris: CNOUS, 1993. A handbook to student life in France.
Giammeralla, Michael. *A Guide for Students Planning to Study in the French University.* Washington, D.C.: NAFSA, 1994. Includes discussion of admission and financial aid procedures, together with information on living accommodations.
Grant, Mary Ann. "Studying in the French University: A Guide for U.S. Advisers and Students." Washington, D.C.: NAFSA, 1990.
"Grants and Fellowships Available for Graduate Study or Advanced Research in France." New York: French Cultural Services (FCS), 1993.
"Studies in France." New York: FCS, 1993. Describes admission procedures and lists universities, including American ones, in France.

For language study:

Repertoire des centres de formation. Paris: Ministère des Affaires Etrangères, Sous-direction de la cooperation linguistique et éducative, 1993. Describes general, specialized, and teacher training courses throughout France by region and city.

GERMANY

For higher education:

Handbuch der Universitäten und Fachhochschulen Bundesrepublik Deutschland, Österreich, Schweiz, 6th ed. Munchen: n.p., 1993. Directory of colleges and universities in Germany, Austria, and Switzerland.
Market, Axel. "Studying in the German University: A Guide for U.S. Advisers and Students." Washington, D.C.: NAFSA, 1990.
Postgraduate Courses in the Federal Republic of Germany, 3d ed. Bonn: German Academic Exchange Service, 1992.

For information on study and research:

German Academic Exchange Service
(Deutscher Akademischer Austauschdienst-DAAD)
950 Third Avenue, 19th floor
New York, NY 10022

GREAT BRITAIN

For higher education and financial aid:

British Council. *"Postgraduate Study and Research at British Universities and Col-
leges."* Describes graduate study in Great Britain, outlining cost, structure, ad-
mission, and living conditions. Lists all British universities with addresses and
communication numbers.
British Universities Guide to Graduate Study. London: Association of Commonwealth
Universities, 1992.
Commonwealth Universities Yearbook, 1993. London: Association of Commonwealth
Universities, 1993. Lists all English-language universities outside the United
States.
Current Research in Britain. Boston Spa, England: British Library Lending Division,
1985.
*Graduate Studies 1994–95: The Complete Guide to over 10,000 Postgraduate Courses
in the UK.* Cambridge, England: Hobsons Publishing, 1994.
The Potter Universities Guide, 3d ed. Huddersfield, England: Dalebank, 1990.
*The Student Book 84–85: The Applicant's Guide to UK Colleges, Polytechnics and Uni-
versities*, 6th ed. London: Macmillan, 1984.
*Studying and Living in Britain, 1993: The British Council's Guide for Overseas Students
and Visitors.* Plymouth, England: Northcote House, 1993.

For information on study and research:

Education Information Section
The British Council
Medlock Street
Manchester, M15 4PR
England, U.K.

ITALY

For higher education:

Boga, Cesare. *Guida alla scelta della facoltà e del corso de laurea*, 31st ed. Milan:
Pirola, 1990.
Sartoratti, G. *Scuole di specializzazione presso le università in Italia.* Padua: Alborg,
1991.
*Annuario DEA [Diffusione Edizioni Anglo-americane] delle università e istituti di studio
e ricerca in Italia-DEA Directory of Universities, Scientific and Cultural Institutions in Italy.* Rome: DEA Editrice, 1989.

JAPAN

For higher education and financial aid:

Asian Students Cultural Association. "Japanese Universities: Graduate Programs for Foreign Students." Tokyo: Dobunkan Shuppan, 1992. Includes table of fields of study and universities offering them.
"Educational Opportunities in Japan." [Washington, D.C.]: Embassy of Japan, 1993. Has extensive section on financial aid for university study or research in Japan. Besides higher education, also has information on high school exchange and Japanese language courses. Includes bibliography of works informing about education in Japan.
Federation of Japanese Private Colleges and Universities Associations [sic] FJPCUS. "Special Courses for Foreign Students in Japanese Private Universities." Tokyo: FJPCUS, 1992.

For language study:

Association for the Promotion of Japanese Language Education (APJLE). "1992 Japanese Language Institutes in Japan." Tokyo: APJLE, 1992.

SCANDINAVIA

For higher education, financial aid, and language study:

Study in Scandinavia: 1994–95, 13th edition. New York: American-Scandinavian Foundation, [1994]. Describes summer and academic year courses in humanities, social sciences, and technical courses at institutions in Denmark, Finland, Iceland, Norway, and Sweden, including availability of financial aid.

SPAIN

For higher education:

Guia de la universidad. Madrid: Ministerio de Educacion y Ciencia, Consejo de Universidades, Secretaria General, 1991.

(In Catalonia)

Guia de l'investigador: institucions i centres públics de serveis a l'activitat de recerca. Barcelona: Generalitat de Catalunya, Comissió Interdepartamental de Recerca i Innovació Tecnològica, 1991.

OTHER SOURCES

In *Film and Video Resources for International Educational Exchange* by Lee Zeigler, several titles are of interest in relation to the above countries: *Favourable Exchange: International Students in Canada, Study in Canada, Foyer international d'accueil de Paris, Briefing on Britain: The Undergraduate Experience,* and *Year Program in Scandinavia.*

For searching works by author, title, and, in most cases, subject, the equivalent of *Books in Print* is available annually for various countries. These reference works include publishers' addresses.

France

Livres disponibles-French Books in Print 1994 (Paris: Editions du Cercle de la Libraire, 1993). In four volumes, two for authors, two for titles. Covers all publishing in Francophone world.

Germany

Verzeichnis Lieferbarer Bucher-German Books in Print 93/94. (Frankfurt: Verlag der Buchandler-Vereinigung, 1993). In seven volumes with author, title, and subject interfiled.

Great Britain

Whitaker's Books in Print (1994) (London: Whitaker Bibliographic Services, 1994). In five volumes with author, title, and subject interfiled.

Italy

Catalogo dei libri in commercio 1994 (Milan: Editrice Bibliografica, 1994). In three volumes, one each for authors, titles, and subjects.

Spain

Libros españoles en venta, 1994. Madrid: Agencia Española del ISBN, 1994. In three volumes, one each for authors, titles, and subjects.

Appendix C

OSEAS Code of Ethics

Within the context of their particular professional situation, advisers should:

1. Provide accurate, complete, current, and unbiased information to the general public at regular, specified times.
2. Use office, title, and professional associations only for the conduct of official business.
3. Ensure that any statements of personal opinion or judgments are clearly designated as such.
4. Clarify the adviser's role to all parties and limit advice to matters within that mandate, making appropriate referrals when necessary.
5. Know and comply with the laws, regulations, and policies of the United States and of the host country.
6. Demonstrate cross-cultural sensitivity, treating differences between U.S. and host country educational systems and cultures non-judgmentally.
7. Respond to all inquiries fairly, equitably, and professionally, respecting the confidentiality of the adviser-advisee relationship.
8. Encourage advisees in an honest and unbiased manner to make a realistic assessment regarding the chances of obtaining appropriate education or training in the United States and the potential problems involved in successful personal and professional re-entry into the home country.
9. Facilitate, when appropriate within the scope of the adviser's job responsibilities or authority, suitable academic placement, avoiding the guarantee of specific placements or financial awards.
10. Refrain from giving names of advisees to third parties, such as colleges, universities, or other agencies or organizations, without the advisees' consent.
11. Refuse reimbursement for expenses and fees for professional services such as lectures or consultations for activities that imply endorsement of particular groups or programs.

12. Decline gifts offered for services rendered, always understanding the full implications attached to such gifts.
13. Understand ethical recruiting and placement practices and support only those organizations or institutions which follow them.
14. Refuse payment from or contractual arrangements with receiving institutions for referral or placement of students.
15. Demonstrate impartiality when facilitating visits by recruiters.
16. Ensure that any promotional materials available in the advising office represent accredited programs, or if accreditation is unavailable, represent programs of established quality.

Bibliography

The following bibliography is a list of works consulted either for the composition of this book or recommended for further reading. Insofar as there are not many bibliographies for international education advising, this one contributes to increasing such resources, giving special focus to library and information science materials relevant to it.

Abed, Joanne. "Concepts of Quality and Ranking." *Overseas Educational Adviser's Manual*. Washington, D.C.: College Entrance Examination Board, 1987, pp. 5/16–22.

Althen, Gary L. *The Handbook of Foreign Student Advising*. Yarmouth, Maine: Intercultural Press, 1984.

Asantewa, Doris. *Strategic Planning Basics for Special Libraries*. Washington, D.C.: Special Libraries Association, 1992.

Berdie, D. R. et al. *Questionnaires: Design and Use*. Metuchen, N.J.: The Scarecrow Press, 1986.

Birke-Dexheimer, Brigitte. "Advising by Mail and Telephone." *Overseas Educational Adviser's Manual*, pp. 2/14–19.

Cassell, Kay Ann, and Elizabeth Futas. *Developing Public Library Collections, Policies, and Procedures*. New York: Neal-Schuman, 1991.

Chambers, Jennifer. "Ranking Colleges and Universities." *The Advising Quarterly* 12 (Spring 1990), pp. 1–4.

The Chicago Manual of Style, 14th ed. Chicago: University of Chicago Press, 1993.

Christianson, Elin B. et al. *Special Libraries: A Guide for Management*, 3d ed. Washington, D.C.: SLA, 1991.

Cochran, J. Wesley. *Time Management Handbook for Librarians*. Westport, Conn.: Greenwood Press, 1992.

Dewey, Melvil. *Dewey Decimal Classification and Relative Index*, 20th ed., four vols. Albany, N.Y.: Forest Press, 1989.

Epstein, Laura. *Talking and Listening: A Guide to the Helping Interview*. St. Louis: Times/Mosby, 1985.

Fallgatter, Juleann S. et al. *Guide to Educational Advising Resources*. Washington, D.C.: AMIDEAST, 1992.

Garten, Edward D., ed. *Using Consultants in Libraries and Information Centers*. Westport, Conn.: Greenwood Press, 1992.

Gordon, Virginia N. *Handbook of Academic Advising*. Westport, Conn.: Greenwood Press, 1992.

Hopkins, John D. "Technology and Change: A Turning Point for Overseas Advising." *The Advising Quarterly* 16 (Spring 1991), pp. 1, 13–17.

———. "Who and What Is an Overseas Adviser? And Why Does It Matter?" *The Advising Quarterly* 26 (Fall 1993), pp. 5–11.

Jackson, Eugene B., ed. *Special Librarianship: A New Reader*. Metuchen, N.J.: The Scarecrow Press, 1980.

Jennerich, Elaine Zaremba, and Edward J. Jennerich. *The Reference Interview as a Creative Art*. Littleton, Colo.: Libraries Unlimited, 1987.

Katz, William A. *Introduction to Reference Work*, 6th ed., 2 vols. New York: McGraw-Hill, 1992.

Kohl, David F. *Acquisitions, Collection Development, and Collection Use*. Santa Barbara, Calif.: ABC-Clio Press, 1985.

Koontz, Harold. "The Management Theory Jungle Revisited." *The Academy of Management Review* 5, no. 2 (April 1980), pp. 175–87.

Machlup, Fritz. *The Production and Distribution of Knowledge in the United States*. Princeton, N.J.: Princeton University Press, 1962.

Magrill, Rose Mary, and John Corbin. *Acquisitions Management and Collection Development in Libraries*. Chicago: ALA, 1989.

Mallery, Mary S., and Ralph E. DeVore. *A Sign System for Libraries*. Chicago: ALA, 1982.

Managing Small Special Libraries, 1992: An SLA Information Kit. Washington, D.C.: SLA, 1992.

Michel, Gillian, and Roma Harris. "Evaluating the Reference Interview: Some Factors Influencing Patrons and Professionals." *RQ* 27 (Fall 1987), pp. 95–105.

Miller, Heather S. *Managing Acquisitions and Vendor Relations*. New York: Neal-Schuman, 1992.

Molsa, Terhi. "Telecommuting and the International Educator." *The Advising Quarterly* 26 (Fall 1993), pp. 1–6.

Moulton, Lynda W. *Data Bases for Special Libraries: A Strategic Guide to Information Management*. Westport, Conn.: Greenwood Press, 1991.

Mount, Ellis. *Special Libraries and Information Centers: An Introductory Text*. New York: Special Libraries Association, 1983.

Murfin, Marjorie, and Lubomyr R. Wynar. *Reference Service: An Annotated Bibliographic Guide*. Littleton, Colo.: Libraries Unlimited, 1977.

———. *Reference Service: An Annotated Bibliographic Guide Supplement, 1976–1982*. Littleton, Colo.: Libraries Unlimited, 1984.

Piercy, Esther J. *Commonsense Cataloging: A Manual for the Organization of Books and Other Materials in School and Small Public Libraries*. New York: H. W. Wilson, 1965.

Porat, Marc Uri. *The Information Economy*, 9 vols. Washington, D.C.: Department of Commerce, 1977.

Prytherch, Ray. *Information Management and Library Science: A Guide to the Literature.* Aldershot, England: Gower, 1994.

Riedinger, Edward A. "An Audio-Visual Manual for Using College Catalogs." *The Advising Quarterly* 1 (Summer 1987), p. 17.

———. "The Beginnings of OSEAS," *AR–OSEAS* (October–December 1989), pp. 5–6.

———. "Collection Development for Overseas Educational Advising." *The Advising Quarterly* 14 (Fall 1990), pp. 1, 18–19.

———. "Computer Uses for Overseas Counseling." *IIE Counselor's Newsletter* (October 1984), pp. 33–34.

———. " 'Information Age' as a Descriptor." *Scholarly Publishing* 21, no. 1 (October 1989), pp. 45–51.

———. "Publishing Overseas Educational Advising Newsletters." *IIE Counselor's Newsletter* (October 1985), p. 23–24.

———. "U.S. Exchange and Librarian Education in Latin America." *AR-OSEAS* (July–September 1989), pp. 6–7.

———. "Use of Videotape and Alumni in Counseling in Brazil." *IIE Counselor's Newsletter* (Spring 1983), pp. 5–6.

Sager, Donald J. *Small Libraries: Organization and Operation.* Fort Atkinson, Wis.: Highsmith Press, 1992.

Schackman, Dulcie, and Ed Battle. "The Three R's of Volunteers: Recruitment, Retention, Recognition." *The Advising Quarterly* 17 (Summer 1991), pp. 1, 5–7.

Sears, Minnie Earl. *Sears List of Subject Headings*, 15th ed. New York: H. W. Wilson, 1994.

Sharp, Harold S., ed. *Readings in Special Librarianship.* New York: The Scarecrow Press, 1963.

Thomson, Marti. "Current Practise in Charging for Educational Advising." *The Advising Quarterly* 18 (Fall 1991), pp. 1, 6–8.

———. "Establishing a Volunteer Advising Program." *The Advising Quarterly* 17 (Summer 1991), pp. 1, 3–4.

Viladas, Joseph M. *The Book of Survey Techniques.* Greenwich, Conn.: Havemeyer Books, 1982.

Widdows, Richard et al. "The Focus Group Interview: A Method for Assessing Users' Evaluation of Library Service." *College and Research Libraries* 52, no. 4 (July 1991), pp. 352–59.

Zeigler, Lee. *Film and Video Resources for International Educational Exchange.* Washington, D.C.: NAFSA, 1992.

Index

For acronyms not explained below, please consult the list of abbreviations (p. xvii).

About the Author

EDWARD A. RIEDINGER is Bibliographer for Latin America at the University Libraries and Adjunct Assistant Professor of History at Ohio State University. He is the former head of the educational advising services of the Fulbright Commission in Brazil, where he pioneered standards for advising collections, adviser training, and the global professional organization of overseas advisers.